TIME

AND

MONEY

YOUR GUIDE TO
ECONOMIC FREEDOM

TIME

AND

MONEY

KENDRICK MERCER

AND

ALBERT GOERIG

Olympia, WA

Disclaimer
This book is designed to provide accurate and authoritative information. This information is obtained from sources and data considered to be reliable, but its accuracy and completeness are not guaranteed by the authors. This book is sold with the understanding that the authors and publisher are not engaged in rendering financial, legal, accounting, or other professional services. If expert assistance is required, the services of a professional should be sought. The authors and publisher specifically disclaim any liability or loss that is incurred as a consequence of the use or application, directly or indirectly, of any information presented in this book.

Published by ACG Press
3424 43rd Ave. S.E.
Olympia, WA 98501

Publisher's Cataloguing-in-Publication Data
Mercer, Kendrick.

      Time and money : your guide to economic freedom / Kendrick Mercer and
      Albert Goerig. — Olympia, WA : ACG Press, 2004.

      p. ; cm.
      Includes index.
      ISBN: 0-9753339-0-9

      1. Financial security. 2. Finance, Personal. 3. Quality of life. I. Goerig, Albert.
      II. Title.

HG179 .M47 2004   2004104381
332.024/01--dc22   0406

Book production and coordination by Jenkins Group, Inc. • www.bookpublishing.com
Editor: Nancy Grimley Carleton
Interior design: Paw Print Media/Debbie Sidman
Cover design: Kelli Leader

Printed in the United States of America.
08 07 06 05 04 • 5 4 3 2 1

About the Cover Illustration

The two coins on the front cover were minted 2,300 years apart and remind us that money has been an important factor in humanity's cultural imprinting throughout the centuries. These two coins were selected because they represent two values needed to reach financial freedom. One is courage and the other is the desire for freedom. The coin on the left is a Greek silver tetradrachm, and was minted sometime between 323 and 281 B.C.E. in the Kingdom of Thrace (the northern part of ancient Greece).

The coin depicts the head of Alexander the Great (356–323 B.C.E.), who died at the age of thirty-three after conquering the known world. He was one of history's most courageous and charismatic leaders. Any man in his army would lay down his life for Alexander in a heartbeat. In those days, soldiers faced their enemies on the battlefield. As his enemies watched, Alexander would stand in front of his thirty-five thousand troops just before battle. Without saying a word, he would drop his toga to complete silence. Alexander was a strong and handsome man, but the front of his body was covered with battle scars because he always led his troops into combat. After displaying the scars on the front of his body, Alexander would turn around to show that he didn't have a single scar on his back, proof that he had never retreated in battle. Following this display, his soldiers would let out a deafening cheer while hammering their shields and swords together in a frenzy. The enemy would quake, and the battle was won before it even started.

The walking liberty half-dollar represents our desire for freedom and liberty. These coins are a reminder that following the philosophy promoted in *Time and Money*, and living a free and beautiful life, takes courage and the intent to break through the fears and cultural imprints that prevent us from experiencing life fully.

Life is a process, not an end;
if you don't enjoy the process,
you'll hate the end!
This book is dedicated
to all who have the courage
to live their own life process.

K. M.

Contents

Part Two: Time: Living with Simplicity

Foreword

For most of my life I have lived the American dream. I got married, had children, and built a successful career. As I moved into my forties, I began to realize that my particular American dream was laced with complications. I was filled not with peace and contentment but with anxiety and a gnawing sense that somehow I was missing out on the real key to living my dream.

I set out on a quest to find the path to true happiness and fulfillment. I eagerly consumed self-help books and tapes from teachers such as Wayne Dyer, Dan Millman, Elaine St. James, Suze Orman, Greg Stanley, John Cummuta, and many others. As I integrated their teachings into my day-to-day life, I found myself experiencing greater peace and tranquility.

One teacher in particular, a man by the name of Kendrick (Rick) Mercer, had a particularly profound effect on the way I looked at time and money—two of the most significant markers of how we experience life. I first heard one of his tapes in 1985, and by the time I met him in the mid-1990s, Rick already had decades of experience as a financial consultant and personal growth facilitator behind him. As Rick reminds us, "Life is a process, not an end; if you don't enjoy the process, you'll hate the end!" So many of us in this culture focus on the end result instead of enjoying the moment.

Rick's approach in dealing with time and money stood out as the essence of simplicity—remarkably easy to learn and apply in my daily life. Once I mastered his simple philosophy, I found I was able to live my life with grace and peace no matter what challenges I encountered.

Rick graduated from law school in 1961; in 1971 he founded his own law firm specializing in financial tax law. The purpose of this firm was to coach professionals, especially doctors, on achieving economic freedom while learning to enjoy their practices, empower their staff, and become better leaders. In 1988, Rick sold the company, which is now known as Mercer Advisors, and started offering personal growth training, first known as Life Mastery and now called the Garden Company. He found that it was easy to help people achieve financial independence, but he also observed that money alone did not make them happier or more at peace. Through the personal growth seminars he has offered over the past sixteen years, Rick has helped his clients find greater serenity and integrity in their lives as they integrate economic freedom with the quest for inner peace.

Rick has a special way of relating very profound ideas through entertaining stories and poignant anecdotes. He conveys basic financial principles in straightforward, easy-to-grasp language. It's always a pleasure to hear him speak and share his powerful wisdom. Up to this point, however, he hasn't written a book, even though he has been speaking and teaching in private workshops and seminars for over forty years.

The purpose of this book is to introduce Rick's philosophy of economic freedom and personal happiness to a wider audience, as well as to give those who've had the good fortune of hearing him in person or on tape a compact reminder for ongoing review and guidance.

My part in the collaboration of writing *Time and Money* was to synthesize the transcripts from recorded tape presentations of Rick's talks over the years and to help shape his various writings into manuscript form. I also contributed research for the money section and specifics about developing a game plan for financial freedom. Once all of this was in place, Rick and I worked to complete the final draft.

In this book, you'll find a specific game plan to help you reach economic freedom and to savor every precious moment of your life to the fullest. *Time and Money* offers a philosophy of life as well as stories and specific guidelines to aid your quest for economic abundance and a healthy relationship to time, as well as insights to help you simplify your life. The rewards are many, but most of all, I urge you to enjoy the process!

Dr. Albert C. (Ace) Goerig
Olympia, Washington

Preface

In the United States of America, we make more money and accumulate more possessions than the vast majority of people in the world. In my more than forty years as a financial advisor, I have worked with people who make millions of dollars a year as well as those who make less than $20,000 a year. All of these people have one thing in common: economic stress. Whether a person makes millions or only a modest amount, no one seems to feel secure about money, let alone at peace with it. Almost everyone experiences some degree of anxiety over present and future economic prospects.

Most of us cannot even imagine experiencing economic peace of mind. What would it be like to live without economic stress? What would it be like to be content with what we have and secure in knowing we can meet whatever challenges life brings our way? What would it be like to live with integrity in the moment, doing only what we truly want to be doing and letting go of the rest?

Some people think that if they had just the right answers, just the right financial advice, their economic stress would go away. But this doesn't seem likely when 20 percent of the service professionals in the United States are paid to give economic answers! If you want to locate economic answers, simply look in the telephone book under stockbrokers, insurance agents, attorneys, accountants, financial planners, estate planners, actuaries, bookkeepers, tax consultants, or real estate agents. The answers these professionals provide, however, will never bring you economic peace.

In *Time and Money*, I share with you a solid context (that is, a clear framework) and a simple game plan that will result in your economic peace of mind. You will learn the secret to economic freedom, which I define as being debt free and having enough safe, liquid assets to reproduce your lifestyle income every year for the rest of your life without touching the principal. And you can easily achieve being debt free in seven to nine years and economically free within fifteen to twenty years by following the basic principles I outline in this book.

In addition to setting you on the path to financial independence, *Time and Money* reveals a new way of looking at time that will free you to enjoy every day of your life to a degree you may never have dreamed possible. By simplifying your life and reaping the fruits of doing only what has meaning to you, you will be living in integrity with both time and money, two of the most important ingredients for experiencing true peace and happiness.

Welcome to the process, and enjoy!

Kendrick (Rick) Mercer
Lake Pend Oreille, Idaho

Acknowledgments

Our deepest appreciation to the following people who contributed, directly or indirectly, to this manuscript: Greg Stanley for his review of the book and brokers Bill Schlofman from A. G. Edwards and Tom Puentes from Smith Barney for sharing their expertise in bonds.

Special thanks to our editor Nancy Grimley Carleton for her skills in developing the format of this book and to Rebecca Chown for the final review. I would like to thank the Jenkins Group for their talented staff of experts, including Leah Nicholson and Kelli Leader, who helped make this book possible.

Rick Mercer and Ace Goerig

PART ONE

Money: Living in Economic Freedom

CHAPTER 1

Finding Economic Peace of Mind

As I mentioned in the Preface, in my forty years as a financial advisor I have worked with everyone from those making a modest annual salary to millionaires. And, sadly, one common theme stands out: no matter how much money they make, and no matter how many investments they have, most people experience a great deal of financial uncertainty and stress. A turn of the market or a sudden rise in unemployment could destroy in a moment the fruits of all their hard work. Caught in the American mania to consume and spend, they are constantly insecure no matter how much high-priced financial advice they're getting. The more insecure they are, the greater the risks they take. What is the way out of this anxious state of economic stress? How can we all reach economic peace of mind? To understand what gets in the way, let's consider some of the cultural roots of economic stress.

Cultural Roots of Economic Stress

The truth is, we create our own economic stress at home and in our careers. Until we talk about this phenomenon in cultural terms and understand what is happening, it's impossible to move beyond economic stress.

Culturally, we are taught to spend our income and go into debt no matter how much money we make. If we knew how to break the addiction of creating economic stress, we would be absolutely peaceful about our finances.

Just imagine what it would have been like during the last ten years of your life if you were debt free and had experienced no economic stress. The feeling of peace would have been a bit like the last day of a year in grade school or high school when you had a summer ahead of you with nothing to do except be free to enjoy the next three months. Can you remember that kind of freedom and peace? With the right approach, this is what your life can be like now.

Instead, we have learned to live within a tight economic envelope no matter how much money we are earning. Look back at your very first job after you finished your education and remember how much money you were making. You can probably recall thinking that if only you could make a certain amount more, you would feel great. But what you make now, years later, is probably much more than what you made back then, and you're still not free of economic stress. As your income goes up, you spend more, so there is a direct ratio of increased economic tension. It's not about how much you make or how much you accumulate. It's the way you're thinking and the context you have about money.

Economic Freedom

In order to move toward a healthier, more satisfying economic life, it's important to understand some basic concepts. The most central of these is *economic freedom*, with the emphasis on the word *freedom*. I define economic freedom as the day we have accumulated enough safe, liquid assets that these assets can reproduce our lifestyle income (the amount of money it takes to maintain our lifestyle), with safeguards against inflation, for the rest of our lives without touching the principal.

The exact dollar amount of economic freedom differs for each individual. For example, economic freedom for a single mom making $24,000 a year would be when she has stored up enough assets to reproduce her $24,000 lifestyle each year without touching the principal for the rest of her life. Once she pays off all her debt, it may only take $12,000 for her to reproduce this $24,000 lifestyle. Economic freedom for a surgeon making $250,000 a year would be when she has stored up enough assets to reproduce her lifestyle every year without touching the principal. Again, once she has paid off all her debt, it will take much less to reproduce her $250,000 lifestyle. In short, economic freedom is the day we go to work because we *want* to, not because we *have* to.

Economic freedom is a mindset of being at peace with the money we have, knowing that we have a clear game plan to follow so that money will never be a concern in our lives. In the classic definition of economic freedom, we leave our heirs the accumulated assets (principal) that was reproducing our lifestyle income. Modifying the definition to include spending and living on these accumulated assets as well as on the interest would allow us to obtain economic freedom five to ten years earlier; in this case, when we die, we might well have spent almost all our money.

Once we have implemented a safe game plan to reach economic freedom, our economic stress will disappear almost immediately. Specifically, if you are thirty years old, you can be financially free by the age forty-five or fifty. What surprises me is simply that everyone isn't doing it!

Financial Freedom for Women

When we look at economic freedom for women in particular, again the central theme is *freedom*, accompanied by its close cousin, *independence*. Many women have bought into the cultural imprint that the man makes most of the money decisions and is the main breadwinner in the family. Other than handling family budgets, many women do not learn about debt reduction, money management, or investing. The sad part is that most men do not understand these concepts either; because of this, both women and men make poor money decisions, resulting in ongoing family stress.

The lack of knowledge about money, along with fear of the unknown, sometimes keeps women in toxic relationships. These women have been told so many times that they cannot survive on their own that they've come to believe it's true. The concepts I'll be teaching in *Time and Money* are very basic and easy to learn. Following them, both women and men can make it on their own and eventually become financially free. With this new knowledge, we can live our lives with greater freedom and independence, which leads to healthier relationships.

This book is especially important for single parents. It will help you come up with an effective game plan for dealing with your money and reaching economic freedom, whether you're a woman or a man.

Your Personal Story and Game Plan

My own financial game plan is comprehensive and designed specifically for my life. It allows me to delight in my home on a beautiful island in Idaho, savoring time with my partner and our garden and animals, as well as to sail, travel, and explore new adventures. In addition, I enjoy my ongoing work as a philosopher, teacher, and seminar leader to the fullest. There is never a moment when this work feels like a burden to me; it is always a choice. It is important to me to have a game plan with integrity that allows money to come into my life and then to flow to my objectives. These objectives include developing enough financial security to do the things I want, the freedom to stop working, the time to nurture my family, the means to send my children to college, a clear way to prioritize what I spend money on, and a simple structure for my financial life. It is also important to me to teach my family to have integrity with money.

What do you want from *your* financial game plan? It is incredibly important to create your own game plan, but first you need to have a new story, which you'll be learning more about in Chapter 5. Unfortunately, too many of us haven't learned how to develop a story about economics. Once you understand the simple definition of economic freedom I've shared in this chapter (having safe, liquid assets that will yield an annual amount to accommodate your lifestyle without touching the principal), you can then build the best context for getting there and eliminating the economic stress in your life. You can define your goals and rewrite a story for your economic life to reach that solution. Then economic peace of mind will be yours, and no one can ever take it away from you.

Economic Peace of Mind

Consider the great Indian leader Mohandas Gandhi. Gandhi lived on the equivalent of three bowls of rice a day, and often he didn't know where his next meal was coming from, yet he had total economic peace of mind. Economic peace of mind is in no way tied to having a particular income, a set number of investments, or a long list of possessions. Someone like Gandhi was content with what he had, even if he didn't know where his next meal was coming from. But for most of us, being on the path to economic freedom provides the security that helps us find true economic peace of mind. For a Gandhi, economic freedom might be when he had stored up enough rice (or knew he had reliable sources for his daily needs) to reproduce three bowls of rice a day for the rest of his life. For you and me, economic freedom is when we have enough invested in safe, liquid assets to yield an income that can sustain our lifestyle for the rest of our lives without touching the principal.

But economic peace of mind is more than just economic freedom. In fact, we can experience economic peace of mind long before we reach economic freedom. Once we have a solid game plan for achieving economic freedom, we can let go of our anxiety about money. With this newfound peace of mind, we can truly enjoy life in the moment because we are secure in what we have and we know that we can deal with any life challenge. We can face life with joy and excitement because we have a vision and a beautiful story for our lives. With *Time and Money*, each of us can claim both economic freedom *and* economic peace of mind.

Tools to Help You Get the Most Out of This Book

For you to reap the most benefits from reading this book, it's crucial that you engage with it, that you put into practice the simple principles and methods you'll be learning. In Appendix A, I have included a number of exercises to help you get the most you can out of *Time and Money*. Please bear in mind that the energy you invest in these exercises will greatly expand the benefits you receive; at the same time, feel free to focus on the exercises that have the most meaning for you and your particular situation and to skip those that don't seem as relevant. You might want to flip back to Appendix A now and do Exercise 1: Creating a Time and Money Journal. The charts and the worksheet in Appendices C through F will also help you in the process of creating a clear game plan for economic freedom. Keeping your Time and Money Journal by your side as you read through the rest of the book will help you turn the ideas in the book into action and set you on the sure path to economic peace of mind.

CHAPTER 2

The Importance of a Clear Context

A *context* is the framework or model we use to live our lives and see our life's potential and possibilities. Culturally, we've learned to be so casual about our money that we don't have any idea how to get out of our economic stress. Instead, we've learned to live with the stress, with no context for an alternative. When we develop a precise, clear context and game plan about how to handle money, the results are incredible and allow us to break the behavioral patterns that have kept us from obtaining economic peace of mind.

In its essence, a clear economic context provides a solid vision of a powerful economic game plan that gives us a way to see exactly where we have been, where we are now, and where we are heading with our finances. Most economic programs are very diffuse and lack power, direction, and clarity. There is very little emphasis on saving and getting out of debt and a larger emphasis on spending. We are led to invest in various assets and to rely on someone else's expertise to tell us when to be "in" or "out" of the market.

Psychologists often say that people won't move out of their current circumstances until they have some kind of context in place that is different from where they currently are because it feels too frightening to jump into the complete unknown. Once a clear context is in place to give us direction, clarity, and power, we can easily formulate a compelling vision, reachable goals, and a solid and meaningful game plan.

Historical Underpinnings

We all experience a multitude of emotions around money, and our fears, worries, and ideas date back thousands, maybe even tens of thousands, of years. At the very beginning of human history, there were very few people. If your family group was threatened by another band, you could always just move because land was abundant. As the human population grew, people organized themselves into tribes; if another tribe tried to take away their land, they could fight or they could decide to leave and find other territory. By the time children were twelve years old, they could always leave the tribe and make a living on their own.

A big transition took place when people formed villages focused around farming in the Tigris-Euphrates Valley (an area that is now known as Iraq). Farming changed people's contexts immediately. While farming added more security to the picture, since grains could be stored in the fat years to get people through the lean years, it also brought a new fear. Since farmers could not move without losing their means of livelihood, fighting became their only choice if another group challenged them. Sure enough, hunter-gatherers recognized farming as a bonanza. If the hunter-gatherers attacked, the farmers no longer had the choice of simply leaving the area, since to do so would mean leaving their farms, so they had to start worrying about how to defend themselves.

In those days, crops came to serve as money; if people owed you something, they would pay you in grain. As civilization advanced, people became more and more specialized, eventually to the point where large numbers were no longer farmers. They might be builders building a wall around the village, soldiers defending the village, or administrators or priests. If the system of exchange didn't work, those who weren't farmers would starve to death because they had to rely upon somebody else for grain. Ever since, civilized people who aren't farmers have worried about money.

Like stored grains, money is the equivalent of stored fat, which is stored energy. When food is short, stored fat keeps us alive until we find more food. As civilization developed, money itself became stored fat. Today, very few of us are farmers. Without money, most of us think we would starve to death because we don't know how to produce enough food to feed ourselves. Today, money is our fat. When we earn money, save it, and invest it responsibly, we create financial and emotional fat, or security. When we can sustain this process reliably—that is, when we have a clear game plan for reaching economic freedom, the point where our stored assets can produce enough income to maintain our lifestyles—we are able to get on with the other meaningful aspects of life.

This is still true today. If the economy declines, we can survive if we have stored money. When we don't have any stored fat in the form of stored money, we become insecure. If we do not have a solid economic game plan and a clear context, we become anxious and worry about debt and whether we will have enough money to get us through. On an unconscious level, we are terrified. If we have no stored money and the economy goes sour, we fear that no one else will support us and we will be broke. How will we live? How will we survive? This is our basic fear. Perhaps we could kick back and trust the government and wait for our Social Security checks to arrive. But I've always found it hard to maintain peace of mind when I put all my trust for my financial future in the hands of the government! Relying on the government is like relying on any outside force; we can easily get the rug pulled out from under us.

Beyond Fight or Flight

Our deeply engrained tribal past has contributed greatly to the volume of stress in our lives. When we were living in small groups and needed to respond to outside dangers in a hostile world, the context of tribal consciousness was critical. In order for us to survive, nature gave us instinctive reactions, such as surges of adrenaline to help us either fight or engage in flight to remove us from danger. When a twig snapped, we would immediately be ready to run or to stay and fight.

In modern life, there is generally less to worry about in terms of immediate dangers to our physical survival. Most of us live in fairly safe circumstances, but our built-in reaction of adrenaline surges continues. Little things happen in our economic life—we bounce a check, or get a parking ticket, or notice a late fee on our credit card bill—and our adrenaline is off and running. We are like yo-yos as we bounce up and down based on these cumulative stimuli.

It can be challenging to move beyond these tribal fight-or-flight reactions, but it is possible to choose a new context. Once I was giving a seminar and I drove my nice new yellow Porsche from Santa Barbara to the meeting site. After the seminar, I walked out to discover that my car had been stolen. But this didn't even bother me. Why would I want to make my life unhappy over it? These things happen, and once we've moved beyond fight-or-flight tribal instincts, we accept circumstances for what they are. True peace comes when we learn to accept the unacceptable. I had a great evening, and then I flew home. Because I had a solid context, I didn't need to let myself be jerked around by the changing vicissitudes of life. But to develop this healthy relationship with money, we first need to free our context of stress-producing illusions.

The Illusion That Money Will Make Us Happy

Most Americans have fallen prey to the illusion that money will make us happy. As mentioned previously, I've worked with many millionaires. There are more miserable, depressed, and anxious millionaires than you can imagine! I've seen in no uncertain terms that money absolutely will *not* buy happiness. Nothing that money can buy will make us happy on an ongoing basis, and many people resent those who have money.

Unfortunately, the belief that money will make us happy seems almost unstoppable. It is one of the big illusions that keeps us from coming into integrity with money. Some people think that if they win the lottery they will be happy, but things never seem to work out that way. Sometimes money can actually make people miserable because of their false expectation of what it will bring. What makes us happy is having integrity in every aspect of our lives, including expressing our feelings through travel, through love, and through relationships.

On some level, we all know that money will not make us happy, but we still act *as if* it will. Money does bring a certain kind of security that we wouldn't otherwise have. With that security, perhaps we can express happiness or enjoy life more consistently. But being economically secure is different from being rich. Happiness comes from enjoying each moment and appreciating everything that comes into our lives. There's no precise dollar amount that translates into this capacity! You'll be learning more about how to develop this gift in Part Two. On the other hand, poor money management (such as having high debts and many creditors) can make us unhappy, and that is one good reason for developing a clear financial context, which is what we'll be doing in Part One. Sometimes it takes buying the things we've always thought we wanted to find out that they alone do not bring happiness.

If you have a clear context about money, you'll rent the boat or vacation home you've dreamed of first, to see if it really does add meaning to your life. In addition, you'll come to see that spending without a clear game plan diffuses and wastes your money and makes it take longer for you to reach financial freedom.

The Illusion of Ownership

In the Mercer dictionary, which is a Webster's dictionary with some of the words crossed out, one word that is crossed out is *ownership*. The illusion of ownership prevents us from dealing with money in a real way. On the deepest level, it goes without saying that we can't really own anything, but somehow we *think* we can. Instead, what we really have is *usership* of everything we own.

Contrast is the essence of vision. The easiest way to see this is to give you an example that shows the extremes. I remember when I was in Sunday school. The preacher used to say "You can't take it with you" before passing the collection plate around so we could give "it" to him. I used to wonder whether the minister could take "it" with him! As I grew older, I came to realize that we don't have "it" even now. When we look at death as an extreme in our lives, we notice that our house, our car, our clothes, and our money truly do not go with us. The good news is that neither do our bills nor our debts!

On a deeper level, we come to see that not even our relationships go with us. When we truly understand this, our vision of life undergoes a profound shift—and our context changes.

Many things enter our lives that we have the ability to use. When we start thinking we own things, what we've really done is to buy into cultural misunderstandings and adopt the wrong context about money.

Remember, money is strictly a symbol. It is just an abstraction. The only reason it has value is because others agree with us that it does. Eventually, we come to think of it as real. In the United States, everyone agrees that money is real. If we lost confidence in it, the value would go down. Indeed, this has happened historically. For example, when the Confederacy attempted to break away from the United States in the Civil War, the Confederate government issued Confederate dollars. Initially, these dollars were highly prized. One hundred dollars of Confederate money would buy one hundred dollars' worth of goods. But as the war went on, Confederate dollars would hardly buy anything because everybody lost confidence in the abstraction.

We create value by agreement, but absolute value doesn't exist; it is just an illusion. Once we realize that it is just an illusion, we can change our attitude toward money and possessions. When we understand that money is only an abstraction of economic power and that we do best putting our money into safe, liquid, compounding abstractions, we can charge our economic battery to make it so powerful that its energy will reproduce the income necessary to sustain our lifestyle for the rest of our lives without touching the principal.

When we start thinking differently, we can develop clarity and a precise context to achieve the precise results we envision.

The No Hope Program to Economic Freedom

I call what I present in this book a *No Hope Program*. This means it is not based on vague hopes or cultural illusions but on tested principles and a philosophy that has been proven to work, time and time again. I will show you a conservative approach to handling your money that is sound, safe, and boring. This approach would have survived every economic downfall since the United States was born, including the Great Depression. I will also show you a step-by-step plan for getting out of debt, including paying off your home in five to nine years, depending on the amount of your mortgage and other debts.

If you do not have a lifetime context for every aspect of money, you will never be secure. Many people cannot even imagine feeling grounded or secure about money. It is a big illusion to think that we have to have a great deal of money to be secure. How you manage your money is much more important than how much money you have. Once you set up the proper context for money management, you can be immediately at peace with your finances.

If you follow the context and game plan I am recommending in this book, then you will invest your money in a safe and boring vehicle with a 5, 6, or 8 percent return. This is a real investment, not a fantasy. You have real money and real interest and a solid return that is safe. This is the way economies run and survive. By setting up your game plan on a real basis, you'll find that your earnings will create an abundance of money for you. These investments will always be there no matter what the economy does. This encourages you to put even more money away, eventually leading you to economic freedom.

Once you have a safe game plan to get you to financial freedom, your anxiety over money stops. When you ignore money, you create more anxiety. People know that money is important, but many do not really treat it as if it's important. Most don't keep track of what they spend or set up a plan to save or prepare for retirement. We need to learn how to treat money with respect. People are afraid to track where they spend and store their money because it is always less than they hope it is. When you have money and spend it with respect and integrity, managing your finances becomes light and easy.

I want to help you to understand some simple fundamentals about money that will ensure you have a clear context for reaching economic freedom. Thus, in *Time and Money*, I share my cumulative knowledge and propose a lifetime context for you to safely handle your money and enjoy economic peace of mind.

CHAPTER 3

Integrity with Money

Our behaviors around money often pull us out of balance and keep us from economic peace of mind. When money is tight, we feel insecure. All too often, to compensate for this insecurity, we buy something we don't need in order to feel better, only adding to our economic stress. On the other end of the spectrum are misers, who never feel they have enough no matter how much money they have in the bank. Regardless of how much they have stored away, they never reach a point where they are at peace with what they have. Both extremes lead to insecurity and stress. Both misers and lavish spenders are out of integrity with money, and in both cases, money exposes underlying issues of self-worth.

Coming into integrity with money is essential if we want to live balanced lives. Integrity entails telling the truth to ourselves and others and behaving in ways that are in alignment with that truth. When we come into integrity with money, we are no longer pulled between the extremes of spending and hoarding. We have a clear context and a solid game plan for the financial aspect of our lives, and thus we can easily tell the difference between economic reality and economic fantasy.

Economic Reality Versus Economic Fantasy

Throughout civilized human history, people have shifted back and forth between economic reality and economic fantasy. In early civilization, people would borrow money to build things or to create trade. They would pay a fairly high rate of interest in order to have some money to use. Then somebody thought up the idea of equities (or stocks), where people would share in the success of a company just by investing in it. The company might go to the West Indies and set up a plantation, while the investors stayed at home in England and still received a complete return on their money. Later someone got the idea of buying scrubland and telling investors it was a plantation; this individual made a great deal of money just by selling a stock that had no real value. This is what I mean by *economic fantasy.* In our current era, an astonishing degree of economic fantasy holds sway.

From your childhood history classes, you may remember hearing about the tulip-buying frenzy of 1636. Let me tell you the story of another fantasy known as the South Sea bubble of 1721. The South Sea Company owned a great deal of land in the West Indies and decided to sell stock in the company. At first the land was sold for a reasonable price. Then the price continued to rise daily. Investors thought this would never end, and the unrealistic increase in stock value went on for about two years. Near the end of the bubble, the price was going up 10 percent a day! Even the king of England and his lords were invested in the company. Then, in 1721, the whole thing collapsed, just as shares were selling for four thousand times their real value.

Bubbles like these represent a full-scale investor mania that drives the stock market to unreasonably high levels. Eventually, the bubble is bound to burst. Something similar happened in 1929, when the market collapsed dramatically following a bubble of high values, marking the beginning of the Great Depression. Bubbles of economic fantasy tend to occur, to lesser or greater degrees, every ten to fifteen years.

One of the most recent examples of these bubbles was the astronomical increase in stock values in the 1990s. Of course, everybody loved it while the value of stocks was going up, but look at what followed. From 2000 to 2003, more money was lost than ever before in human history, even including the destruction of Germany and England during World War II. Hundreds of trillions of dollars were lost during those early years of the new millennium. The NASDAQ went down 64 percent and more. At the height of the market, there was an excellent NASDAQ company whose stock was selling for 144 times its earnings. Now that stock has dropped to $13 a share, which is thirty times the company's earnings. Still overpriced, this is pure economic fantasy.

The Illusion of Hope

Not only do we create a great deal of economic stress in our lives when we succumb to economic fantasy, we also create a great deal of hope. Economic hope includes idle dreams, such as wanting to win the lottery or have a stock double in value. This approach to money and life lacks integrity, since integrity relates directly to what we can influence by our own actions, flowing out of our own personal energy. By its very essence, true integrity can never entail our being mere victims or even lucky recipients of external circumstances.

The cultural belief that we have to hit it rich (as in "Some day my ship will come in") to obtain economic freedom is a form of self-defeating hope. This belief prevents us from committing ourselves to a solid geometric progression with our assets that will create economic freedom in a safe and easy manner. To save our money in safe, liquid assets, we do not need to take risks or engage in false hopes. The problem with hoping to strike it rich is that we diffuse our money and spread it all over. If we act now and concentrate our assets through compounding, we will reach economic freedom without risk and without hope.

When we let go of the illusion of hope, we see things for what they are. We set forth a clear context with a game plan that clarifies both the results we want to see as well as what we need to do to make it happen. In this sense, we can't sit back and "hope for the best." Hope causes us to dilute our resources and slows our approach to the finish line. Having a clear context is the most effective antidote to self-defeating economic fantasies. It demonstrates coming into integrity with money.

Creating Our Own Economic Stress

As we can see from the illusions of hope and economic fantasies so endemic to American culture, we participate in creating our own economic stress, which pulls us further out of integrity with money. Sometimes it seems as if we are programmed in our very DNA to spend everything we make even though we know it doesn't make our lives any happier. If spending all we make doesn't do it, we use multiple credit cards and really push ourselves into stress with debt. I'm reminded of when the Air Force was trying to break the sound barrier. Every time an airplane got near the sound barrier, it would encounter heavy turbulence. The pilot would get the airplane close to breaking through the barrier, but would have to back off every time. Some wondered whether anyone would ever be able to go faster than the speed of sound. Of course, engineers continued to redesign airplanes, but the basic problems persisted: going from peaceful airspace into turbulence, and then into chaos. Finally, the Air Force changed the context and game plan by building bigger planes with more horsepower and wingspans with greater stability, and at long last they blasted through the sound barrier.

Our habits of spend, spend, spend are similar. We approach the barrier of our comfort level, but we keep spending. Then we get tense about money and go into turbulence with even more spending. Some people go as far as chaos, declaring bankruptcy, getting divorced, or changing occupations. Without an organized and efficient context about money, we push against the economic barrier that creates constant stress in our lives, and we don't have a clue about how to break through to a peaceful relationship with money. The game plan I am recommending in *Time and Money* is like a supersonic jet that can safely transport you to a state of peace and integrity with money without all of the turbulence.

Cultural and Family Imprinting

Our attitudes toward money can keep us from living full and peaceful lives. We have all inherited a range of imprints from our families of origin concerning money, often including prejudices, insecurities, and false assumptions, which pull us away from coming into integrity with money. We tend to repeat the clichés about money we learned as children, even if they're not true, such as "You can never have enough money," "It takes money to make money," "The poor working man can never get ahead," and "You have to work hard for your money."

Most people who have plenty of money keep working not because they enjoy it or choose it but because working has come to represent worthiness. It is a kind of cultural fad. For most people, work seems to justify their very right to exist. The family imprint to produce may be incredibly strong, or perhaps work has become an addiction. Many work simply because that is what society expects them to do or because their parents told them they'd be bums if they didn't work hard six days a week. Our current attitudes about money tend to limit our choices even once we have plenty of wealth.

The ideal balance would be to have a great deal of money and at the same time to be at peace doing only what we really want to do.

The Importance of Saving

Setting money aside is what we call *saving money*. Some people think that they simply don't make enough money to be able to save. This idea originates from integrity with money. We don't necessarily have to make a great deal of money, but to reach economic peace of mind we have to treat the money we do make with respect. We need to save money. It is essential to set some money aside to create a safety net in case something happens, such as a medical emergency, a car breaking down, or retirement. Remember how ancient farmers stored part of their harvest in the fat years so they could survive the lean years? Saving money creates financial and emotional fat. In Chapter 7, I'll show you how to make saving money a key part of your economic context. All great savers have changed their mindset to believe that they have no choice but to save.

In contrast, never feeling like there will be enough leads to the most reckless blunder of all: speculation. Risking hard-earned, carefully saved money in speculative investments generally results in harsh lessons. Most speculative investments lose money. It is better to avoid this pitfall altogether, especially if you feel as if you will never be able to save enough.

Once you have safely stored what you need for financial and emotional fat, it is okay to set aside a small gambling fund and to speculate with it. But let's be truthful about gambling: taking risks with any of your money leads to anxiety. It feels great when your investment is going up, but terrible when it is going down. There's a palpable tension and insecurity when people lose their money in the stock market or other investments. It's okay to have fun with money and even gamble with some as long as it's enjoyable, but being addicted to such gambling lacks integrity. Never gamble with your retirement money.

The very nature of economic trends is to fluctuate up and down. When we have a solid context for money, we are not subject to these trends and we do not act on temptation. In the 1990s, people were throwing all of their money into the stock market because you "couldn't lose." Whenever you hear that you can't lose, it's a sure sign losing is about to happen! Observing the historical trends of the market helps us see this point. Once we come into integrity with money, saving and investing wisely rather than speculating becomes the heart of our economic context.

Beyond Economic Freedom

During my forty years as a financial advisor and tax attorney, I've had people come to see me from all over the country for economic reasons, but many were also seeking a philosophy about how to live life. From the beginning, in my heart I knew I wanted to inspire people to move beyond economic survival so they could truly thrive in their lives, but initially I did not know how to do it. I thought that if I could help people reach economic freedom, they would not have to worry about money and they would naturally focus on living more fulfilled lives.

What I found was that the clients who did not have a proper economic context got worse as they started to accumulate wealth. The more money they had, the more concerned and worried they became. What I realized was that before they could be at peace with money, they had to open up and address some of the deeper behavioral issues that were keeping them from having integrity with money and with life.

As the clients who had changed their negative family imprints and had a good context got closer to economic freedom, their openness to examining how they were living their lives grew. They loosened their death grip on their businesses. They became more willing to incorporate my suggestions on creating win-win relationships with their employees, such as paying them well and making sure their employees had opportunities for economic freedom. I also showed my clients the benefits of never working with someone they didn't like.

Establishing a solid philosophy or context about money that amplifies balance is the hallmark of integrity. The simpler and clearer our economic context, the more beautifully we can live. Our culture has created too much complexity around money, a topic that craves to be handled with simplicity. When we get complex, we confuse ourselves and lose power. I live a very simple life, but it is a very powerful one. To really live a beautiful life story, we need to come into integrity with money. This requires moving beyond family and cultural scripts and illusions, adopting a clear, effective context for our economic lives, and telling ourselves the truth about economics. In order to have integrity with money, we need to set up a context and model for handling money safely and systematically. Once we own this context, we can then realize that many of our old family patterns and imprints around money simply do not work.

CHAPTER 4

Exploring Family Patterns and Money Scripts

Economics represents survival for most people. We try to move beyond survival, but many of us don't succeed because of our attitudes and beliefs about money and how it works. Yes, money is important for survival and gives us some degree of security, but when we are always worried about money, we are not free to express ourselves in ways that are in alignment with our deepest truths. Most people have emotional and psychological issues around money. Coming into integrity with money is fairly simple, but cultural messages, societal values, family imprints, prejudices, and internalized beliefs often hold us in their sway. You may think your attitudes about money are healthy, but they probably are not. Our cultural and family prejudices are carried into every aspect of our lives, and they tend to trigger us and to affect how we spend and invest money. We get a majority of these imprints and attitudes from our families of origin.

Family Scripts about Money

Many parents say to their children, "Look how hard I've worked so that you can have money" or "Look what I'm sacrificing for you." These messages create guilt and shame around money. Many children grow into adulthood with a vague and confusing concept of money. When money is not talked about openly in the family, this magnifies its important and amplifies our level of tension. We develop all kinds of weird fears around finances, thinking that we might lose all our money or that it has to be hard to make money. Because we have this economic fear and anxiety, any time there is a problem in our relationships, or whenever we have some other life crisis, money issues come right to the top. This is especially true in the case of a death or divorce in the family. The tension has been there all the time, but it was lying just beneath the surface.

Some examples of family imprints and attitudes around money include:

You shouldn't tell others how much money your family has.

People shouldn't flaunt their money.

You are a bum if you don't work hard six days a week.

Men should make more money than women.

You need to work.

Poor people are closer to God.

Don't talk about money.

You should only get paid for things you don't enjoy.

Money doesn't grow on trees.

Money is hard to get.

Money isn't everything.

The man should be the provider for the family.

One day your ship will come in.

It's shameful to lose money.

Another depression might be coming.

Don't talk about where money comes from.

Too much is never enough.

Rich or poor, it's nice to have money.

You can never be too rich or too thin.

Rich people aren't happy.

Time is money.

Money talks.

Money is power.

Rich people oppress poor people.

Don't have more than you need.

Money is the root of all evil.

It takes money to make money.

Poverty is awful.

Give and you shall receive.

How did they get their money?

You're just lucky to have money.

You got your money when someone died.

Expressions such as "dirty money," "old money," "nouveau riche," "trust fund baby."

These prejudices and attitudes, and the shame and judgment associated with them, are carried into our lives and tend to control the way we handle our money. If you have shame around money and you start earning more, your guilt will cause you to behave unconsciously to get rid of or to hide it. I know millionaires who drive old cars just so no one will question them about their money.

Most of our childhood pain around money stems from issues of control. Parents sometimes hold back money when children are "bad" or do not get good grades. It's just as damaging when they reward children with money for "being good." In either case, these are attempts at control based on fear of abandonment or other forms of rejection or conditional acceptance. When we are born, we just want to be loved for who we are, unconditionally, for no reason whatsoever. Control expressed through money has led to a culture of people with extreme money disorders.

If your parents did not know how to give affection and love, they may have used money as a substitute. When money serves as a substitute for love and nurturing, children grow to adulthood and cannot figure out why they are so needy where money is concerned. The reason is that, to them, money equals love.

We cannot change our emotional past concerning money until we have knowledge. We tend to unconsciously sabotage our own success if we believe that rich people are bad or that work has to be hard to be good. This is especially true if we do not feel we deserve wealth.

My family of origin was poor during my childhood, and my mother left. She met a rich man with an airplane and took off with him. I can't blame her for going after money, but this meant money took on a special significance for me. For many years, I gave myself away to money, but finally I took myself back by coming to terms with my money autobiography. You cannot really have abundance when you give yourself away to money by making it too important. The minute we make anything too important, we begin to struggle with it and create pain around it. When we take ourselves back, we regain our freedom.

You, too, can benefit from exploring your family history around money. Exercises 2 and 3 in Appendix A give you the opportunity to explore your own personal money history, and Exercise 4 will help you begin the process of creating a clear new context for your financial well-being so that you can come into full integrity with money.

CHAPTER 5

Creating a New Money Story

We are here on this planet for a relatively brief period of time, and all we have is from now until the end of our lives. So how can we make the most of this time? To live our lives to the fullest, we need to move into a new vision or story of what is possible. We all have the ability to live the rest of our lives as a very exciting adventure. Because of our cultural context and the lack of training most of us have received regarding financial matters, it is difficult to set up a game plan for reaching financial freedom or even to recognize that our way of relating to money could be very different. When we write a new story about how we want to live, it is easy to develop and follow a game plan to fulfill that new story.

Creating new stories helps us move past our cultural patterns, childhood imprinting, and other behavioral patterns. It is one of the most powerful ways we can grow and move forward in our lives. Stories are really about vision. Most of us haven't known how to develop a coherent and compelling story about economic freedom. Until we can dream a beautiful story, we cannot live it. Nothing happens without a story. This is true for every aspect of our lives. Each person is different and unique, and our uniqueness resides in each of us as individual dreamers. For our stories to be visionary, our dreams need to be in the realm of possibility and in alignment with economic reality.

Creating Beautiful Stories

I like to create beautiful stories that convey what I most admire. Because I was fearful as a child, I admire courage. I thus tend to create stories and engage in activities that require courage. I once sailed across the ocean single-handedly, I have founded multimillion-dollar businesses, and I have created a beautiful story I love to live. All of us have the capacity to tell great stories. I've learned that my stories don't have to come true in every respect for me to be happy. My stories inspire me. They help me take action. They serve as a compass that guides me in the right direction. They act as magnets to bring people, ideas, and resources into my life to support my aspirations. My stories are always win-win scenarios. Once I have a philosophy or code to live by, I can create a story within that framework. My personal code includes the elements of freedom, independence, and self-integrity in a context of sanctuary (a place of safety) empowered by love on a bedrock of truth. Creating a story allows me to expand my life and move out of my comfort zone.

Stories are not about winning or losing or end points but about keeping us in the process of living by giving us direction. Remember, they do not have to come true in every detail. I can dream about building a new house, but if I worry about all of the little things that could go wrong, these worries become the expectations that pull me out of enjoying the moment. The stories I create about building my house, about my relationships, and about my work and my hobbies add to my life. I simply tell beautiful stories and move into each story without expectations. When a story has expectations or end results, we are living materially instead of spiritually, and this takes away from the power of the story.

The best stories are specific *and* flexible—specific in offering a full vision with rich detail, flexible because life is a process and we are always growing. As new experiences arise, we begin to see things at a deeper level. When situations change, we need to give ourselves permission to change our minds to stay within our self-integrity. As Mahatma Gandhi once said, "God is the only one who knows real truth; as a man, I only know relative truth, so I can change my mind when my truth changes."

Creating new stories is almost always a bit risky and scary, since what we dream up comes with the risk that someone else may not like our dream. Once we accept ourselves totally, however, it simply doesn't matter what other people think. When we reach the point where we can't be swayed by others' opinions of what we do or don't do, we are free to dream and free to act on our dreams.

You can create a beautiful story that incorporates abundance into your life. Having your finances in order will help support your positive story so that you can live life fully. However, writing a new life story takes great courage because it involves change. Sometimes there are many things in life you need to change so you can live a free and independent life. In this case, you are called upon to face your fears of confrontation and conflict and to create the life you want. Your story shows the world your intent to change and starts you on your new path.

Although your new life story will include money and prosperity, it's not just about that. It's about changing your attitude toward life, and your new money story will touch on all aspects of your life. As the saying goes, "If you always do what you have always done, you will always get what you have always got." The only way to change what you always get is through intent and action. The action of writing your new story is the most powerful way to make this happen. Exercise 5 in Appendix A guides you through the process of writing your new money story. Your new story will create a positive tension toward movement, which in turn will become the real enjoyment. It is challenging to make changes in our lives, and our stories help keep us on the path. Life is an ever-evolving process. Over time, as we grow and see things at a deeper level, we can modify and rewrite our stories.

When we focus on our new stories, which will include a sound economic plan and the philosophy of economic abundance, we will naturally move out of our old stories and start living our new ones. We will naturally overcome our unconscious, unreasonable fears and walk out of the cloud of negative emotions about money. Once we have new stories that express integrity with money, we have begun a process that allows us to experience true economic peace of mind.

Breaking Behavioral Patterns through Goal Setting

In addition to writing a beautiful story, many people find that goal setting is very important in helping them change their behavioral patterns. When we set goals and read them repeatedly, our subconscious takes these goals on and they become dominant thoughts. This begins to change our entire perspective on life. When we repeat our financial goals over and over to ourselves, eventually we find ourselves believing that we can save and reduce debt.

To help you break your behavioral patterns around money, write each of your goals as a short statement in the present tense that focuses on a specific result and a specific time frame. This might be as simple as saying, "I will save 20 percent of my earned income this year and pay off my credit card debt by [a specific date]." It is important to keep each goal focused on one or two things at the most in order to give your subconscious a clear message. Once you write your goals down and start to repeat them regularly, you will begin to see visible changes in your life. Reading your goals affirms your message to your subconscious. Some people read their goals four or five times a day, while others read them weekly. When you read them long enough and often enough, your identity shifts, changing you from a spender to a saver. Belief eventually manifests as behavior. Writing your goals on three-by-five cards and reading them repeatedly helps your subconscious override self-defeating behaviors. To inspire you toward the goal of paying off your home, take a picture of your home and write down the date it will be paid off. Place this photo on your refrigerator. Then do the same with your car.

Your goals make a strong statement to the world about who you are and where you are going. Like your new money story, they act as magnets to bring into your life all the ideas, people, and tools needed to make them happen. Your goals also serve as a compass on a ship; they allow you as the captain to sail in a specific direction and help you make the changes you need to make to get to your new destination. You find yourself more open to debt reduction and increasing your savings, and more reluctant to spend impulsively and incur monthly payments. You become very creative in coming up with the answers you need to reach your objectives. You find more ways to make more money and fewer ways to spend it.

Make sure that your goals address increasing your income, reducing your spending, and increasing your savings. Some examples of savings goals include:

I am saving 10 percent of my income, and in six months [give a specific date] I will increase my savings to 20 percent of my income.

I will increase my business income by 15 percent by [specific date].

I will pay off all my credit card debt in one year [specific date].

I will pay off my car in two years [specific date].

I will pay off my home in seven years [specific date].

After I pay off my small debt, I will use 10 percent of my income [specific amount] to pay off a large debt and 10 percent of my income [specific amount] for savings.

Additional goals will occur to you as you read the rest of the book. Be sure to note them in your Time and Money Journal and copy them onto three-by-five cards. Read your goals over and over again, and imagine as vividly as you can that you are carrying them out, and in sixty days you will start seeing a payoff. Money will start piling up because you'll forget to buy things!

When you start changing your behavioral patterns around getting out of debt, you may experience a bit of an uncomfortable feeling. Once you've paid off your car and no longer have a car payment, for example, you may experience an uneasy feeling that might even last a few months. Your friends who have not paid off debt may reinforce these uncomfortable feelings. You may find that you need new friends to go with your new money story and your clearer context. The payoff is that having savings tends to bring greater emotional security and makes you happier, while acquisition and having many possessions all too often leads to a sense of emptiness.

How to Change Your Past Behavior and Context

In my old business, I used to have a sign posted that read, "Then the day came when the pain to remain the same exceeded the fear to change." *Pain* and *reward* are motivating factors that help people move beyond the fear of change. When you're changing your context to become a saver rather than a spender, remind yourself of the pain and the feeling of enslavement associated with your debts. For example, feel the pain you associate with working at a place you don't like and doing a job that you hate. In contrast, visualize and feel the reward and joy of living your new life story. Make a list of all the pains and drawbacks of being in debt, and next to it write a list of all of the rewards of becoming financially free. Copy this list into your Time and Money Journal and post this list at home and at work. Review it when you are tempted to return to some of your old spending behaviors. As you work with the principles in *Time and Money,* you are developing a reliable game plan for getting out of debt as well as an investment strategy that is very safe, where you will never lose your principal and will always have a stated amount of return.

Summary of Behavior-Changing Mechanics

1. Stimulate your desire to change by looking at and writing down past pains associated with debt and future rewards.
2. Recognize and acknowledge your spending behaviors and family imprints.
3. Take total responsibility for your actions and the things that come into your life so that you are no longer a victim of your past history.
4. Visualize and write a beautiful new story about your life, focusing on the rewards. Remember the times when you had very little but loved your life.
5. Write specific goals for increasing your income, reducing your debt, and increasing your savings.
6. From now on, stop borrowing money and start paying cash for everything, with the possible exception of a new home or further education.
7. Form an intent and make a commitment in your heart to change. Intent is the laser to the soul.
8. Take action by putting the *Time and Money* game plan into practice today.
9. Take time to learn and thoroughly understand the concepts in this book concerning debt reduction and investing.
10. Review your goals daily or weekly, and redo the numbers monthly.
11. Recognize and acknowledge the feelings of being uncomfortable that are associated with change.
12. Celebrate your successes.

CHAPTER 6

Understanding Geometric Progression

Now that you've created a clear vision for yourself by writing a new money story and setting specific goals, it's time to turn to the key underpinnings of the economic game plan you'll be developing.

Most of us who have had an elementary school education have heard the term *geometric progression,* but very few of us truly understand it. As a financial advisor, I've worked with geometric progression for over forty years and it still continues to amazes me. Albert Einstein, one of the most brilliant mathematicians and physicists who has ever lived, once wrote that even with all of the mathematics he had studied, he still did not understand how compound interest (geometric progression) really functioned. When he worked out the figures, the results were so astonishing it seemed like magic. Geometric progression is like a multifaceted diamond; when we look at it from a different angle, we see new dimensions of its beauty.

For you to internalize the context and game plan that will lead you inevitably toward economic freedom, it is essential that you have a basic grasp of the power of geometric progression. This will allow you to see how tiny differences make vast differences over any sustained period of time when geometric progression is involved.

Metaphors for Understanding Geometric Progression

If we graph a geometric progression, we find that it does not form a steady and constantly increasing line, but rather accelerates exponentially. The farther out we go, the more the line looks as if it is bending back on itself. A metaphor I use to demonstrate the power of geometric progression is that of folding a piece of fine tissue paper 1/1000 of an inch thick many times. Each time we fold it, we are doubling its thickness. When we double it over itself the first time, it is 2/1000 of an inch thick. If we were to complete this doubling process fifty times, the stack of tissue paper would be so high it would reach thirty-six times to the moon and back! This is hard to believe, but it's true. The same principle applies to money invested in a geometrically progressing environment.

Some people think that because we have to wait until the fiftieth fold, or event, to get such an astronomical result, there's no point even bothering to start. What's important to understand is that *the first fold is equal to the last one.* If we don't fold the tissue for the first time, we don't just lose 1/1000 of an inch; we lose eighteen times to the moon and back. If we neglect the first two folds, we lose twenty-seven times to the moon and back. We each have a different number of these metaphorical folds in our economic lives.

An excellent example of geometric progression is compound interest in a tax-deferred environment. A normal arithmetic progression entails simply adding to the principal on a regular basis without adding interest. But when we add interest to a normal arithmetic progression, our money grows extremely quickly (the charts at the end of this chapter will give you a sense of this). I know some clients with moderate portfolios that will grow to close to $4.4 million by retirement. Waiting one year at the beginning to start putting money away at a 6 percent return would cost them over $247,000, because this is what they'd be receiving as one year's interest at the end.

John M. Cummuta in his book *Are You Being Seduced into Debt?* gives the following example of the power of compound interest. If the $24 in beads that purchased the island of Manhattan by the Dutch back in 1626 had instead been placed as cash compounding annually at 8%, it would be worth $272 trillion, which would be sufficient to buy Manhattan as it exists today, with enough left over to purchase a few smaller cities.

On the other side of the equation, when we are paying interest on our debts, instead of receiving the benefits of compound interest, we're at the mercy of one of the most powerful forces on Earth. When we have debt, we are not receiving compound interest; instead, we are paying it, and this powerful force is working against us. That is why it could cost you as much as $598,772 to buy a $250,000 house with a 7 percent thirty-year mortgage (see Chapter 14 for more on why it's a good idea to pay off your house early). The sooner we get out of debt and start to save, the sooner we move to the winning side of the compound interest equation.

Quality Wealth

Geometric progression only works if we don't lose any of the principal. The *Time and Money* game plan calls for quality wealth. Quality wealth is liquid, compounding, safe assets that can survive extreme economic conditions while never losing principal. Most people have their money invested in instruments that lack quality, meaning they would not respond well to every economic condition. They have much of their wealth tied up in land, homes, stocks, and other things that are difficult to sell or that go down in value in tough times. Most of their portfolio would not survive an extreme economic event, such as the Great Depression that started in 1929. During the Great Depression, the drop in the stock market was so extreme that many people went into the tribal consciousness of fight or flight; when the adrenaline hit, some even decided on flight off of high buildings. There were more suicides during the Great Depression than during any other economic downturn.

Remember, if you have liquid assets and an economic depression comes along, your liquid assets become even more valuable. In an economic depression or recession, prices go down. So if you have liquid assets, you have more buying power. Liquid assets are assets that can be sold in a short period of time in any economic condition, such as certificates of deposit (CDs), bonds, or United States treasuries. According to this definition, real estate, businesses, and other property are *not* liquid assets.

To have quality wealth, all we need to do is put some money away every year at a low, safe rate that would survive something equivalent to the Great

Depression, and it will eventually progress geometrically to an incredible amount of money. There are very few of us who understand this concept. We do not have to be getting a big rate of return for this to happen, but we do need to be engaging in the process steadily and without taking any risks that might result in our losing our principal. The steady growth gives us a good result and also gives us absolute confidence that we will not lose.

When we start daydreaming about high-interest, high-risk investments, we get off track from the sound concept of geometric progression. We end up risking what we've already made and sabotage the very process that will set us on the way to economic freedom.

Staying Motivated

To help you stay motivated to stick with the *Time and Money* game plan, I'd like to give you an example of the power of geometric progression. The chart at the end of this chapter provides an example of an individual with annual earnings of $100,000. Over the past thirty years the average return on ten-year treasury bonds has been around 8 percent, and the average return on tax-free municipal bonds has been around 6 percent. In 2004, average returns are about 2 percent lower. The chart shows the interest and ending balance on a portfolio that reflects annual savings and investments of 40 percent of the investor's income in tax-deferred environments (United States treasuries paying 8 percent interest) or tax-free environments (tax-free municipal bonds paying 6 percent interest). Once all of their debts are paid, most people can easily free up 40 percent of their income to invest in their retirement. Looking at the 8 percent side of the chart, we see that after nine years, the interest just about equals annual savings (this line is highlighted in bold). At this point, the interest on these annual savings in a tax-deferred environment provides enough to meet the individual's living expenses at retirement (financial freedom), as you'll see when you read the next section on real retirement needs.

Planning for Real Retirement Needs

When you're working toward economic freedom, an important question to ask yourself is "How much money do I really need in retirement to maintain my lifestyle?" If you're following the *Time and Money* game plan and investing your personal savings in tax-free municipal bonds and your retirement savings in Roth IRAs at 6 or 8 percent, you will be able to withdraw your ending balance entirely tax-free. When the money you earn is tax-free, you need much less to live on. For example, someone earning $30,000 per year in a 15 percent tax bracket would need just $25,500 net income to live on. Someone earning $100,000 in a 27 percent tax bracket would need $73,000 to equal their spent income. Someone earning $250,000 in a 35 percent tax bracket would need $162,500 to equal the buying power of $250,000 in taxable income. Also, remember that in the early years of the twenty-first century, we are paying some of the lowest tax rates of the past sixty years. There is probably a good likelihood that taxes will increase at some point, making tax-deferred retirement plans less valuable, and tax-free income that much more appealing.

MONEY NEEDED FOR RETIREMENT

	A	B	C	D
Current annual income	Minus taxes	Equals this amount	50% of column B needed for retirement	Years after debt is paid to reach economic freedom
$30,000	- $4,500 (15%)	$25,500	$12,750	Year 9.5 (8%)
$100,000	- $27,000 (27%)	$73,000	$36,500	Year 9.5 (8%)
$250,000	- $87,500 (35%)	$162,500	$81,250	Year 8.2 (8%)

If you're following the *Time and Money* game plan, you will be debt free by the time you retire, which will cut your expenses in half. Look at the preceding chart to get a sense of what you will really need to live on at retirement; you'll see that it's only 50 percent of your after-tax income. Most people can reach this stage within fifteen to twenty years, taking into account the years it takes them to become totally debt free. Once you reach this point, you can stop working, take classes at your local college, become self-employed, or do something you always wanted to do. Most people continue to work and make more money because they like what they are doing. Then the money really starts adding up.

Even if you're getting started later in life, once you have consolidated your existing assets and sold the things that no longer add meaning to your life, putting the money into safe, liquid assets, you may be surprised at how close you are to economic freedom. The following chart does not take in consideration pensions and Social Security benefits received after age sixty-two, which could well reduce your retirement needs by another 30 percent, nor does it take into consideration income from part-time work.

Many financial advisors make you think that you need to save much more money then you really need for retirement because they tell you that inflation will make your money worth less at the end. They scare you into buying commission-based investments that carry much higher risk. Over the past forty years, I have observed that the effects of inflation are really negligible because each year our earnings go up correspondingly. If we put 20 percent of that additional salary increase into savings, this protects us from inflation and results in the value of our money at retirement equaling today's dollars.

Using the *Time and Money* game plan to be completely debt free before retirement and to have other large expenses paid for, such as our children's college educations, weddings, and care for elderly parents, allows us to live just as well on 40 to 50 percent of our previous taxable income. When they retire, many people sell their large homes and buy more manageable smaller homes; they then invest the difference, adding to their retirement income. Most Americans also receive Social Security payments and money from retirement plans. According to the 2000 United States Census, the average male retiree over sixty-five years of age lives on about $18,166 per year, and the average couple over sixty-five gets by on $31,568, which is 40 to 50 percent of the income they earned between ages thirty-five and sixty-five. The *Time and Money* game plan gives you a greater comfort margin. When you follow this game plan, you will have so much abundance you'll be able to travel first-class in your retirement. As one of my clients once told me, "If you can afford to go first-class and you don't, your children will!"

The following chart was modified from the Kansas City Life Calculator found online at http://www.fincalc.com/kcl/kclINV02i.htm. You can go to this site and modify it to fit your circumstances, or you can take the $100,000 chart here and multiply it by the appropriate percentage to reflect what you make. For example, if you earn $75,000, then multiply the results in this chart by .75. If you earn $200,000, multiply the results by 2.0. Appendix B also includes charts for those earning $30,000 and $250,000.

SAVING CHART SHOWING GEOMETRIC PROGRESSION OF YOUR SAVINGS

$100,000 Income	Tax-Deferred Savings				Tax-Deferred Savings		
Year	Annual Savings	Beginning balance	Interest 6.00%	Ending balance	Year	Beginning balance	Interest 8.00%	Ending balance
1	$40,000	$40,000	$2,400	$42,400	1	$40,000	$3,200	$43,200
2	40,000	82,400	4,944	87,344	2	83,200	6,656	89,856
3	40,000	127,344	7,641	134,985	3	129,856	10,388	140,244
4	40,000	174,985	10,499	185,484	4	180,244	14,420	194,664
5	40,000	225,484	13,529	239,013	5	234,664	18,773	253,437
6	40,000	279,013	16,741	295,754	6	293,437	23,475	316,912
7	40,000	335,754	20,145	355,899	7	356,912	28,553	385,465
8	40,000	395,899	23,754	419,653	8	425,465	34,037	459,502
9	40,000	459,653	27,579	487,232	**9**	**499,502**	**39,960**	**539,462**
10	40,000	527,232	31,634	558,866	10	579,462	46,357	625,819
11	40,000	598,866	35,932	634,798	11	665,819	53,266	719,085
12	**40,000**	**674,798**	**40,488**	**715,286**	12	759,085	60,727	819,812
13	40,000	755,286	45,317	800,603	13	859,812	68,785	928,597
14	40,000	840,603	50,436	891,039	14	968,597	77,488	1,046,085
15	40,000	931,039	55,862	986,901	15	1,086,085	86,887	1,172,971
16	40,000	1,026,901	61,614	1,088,515	16	1,212,971	97,038	1,310,009
17	40,000	1,128,515	67,711	1,196,226	17	1,350,009	108,001	1,458,010
18	40,000	1,236,226	74,174	1,310,400	18	1,498,010	119,841	1,617,851
19	40,000	1,350,400	81,024	1,431,424	19	1,657,851	132,628	1,790,479
20	40,000	1,471,424	88,285	1,559,709	20	1,830,479	146,438	1,976,917
21	40,000	1,599,709	95,983	1,695,692	21	2,016,917	161,353	2,178,270
22	40,000	1,735,692	104,141	1,839,833	22	2,218,270	177,462	2,395,732
23	40,000	1,879,833	112,790	1,992,623	23	2,435,732	194,859	2,630,590
24	40,000	2,032,623	121,957	2,154,580	24	2,670,590	213,647	2,884,238
25	40,000	2,194,580	131,675	2,326,255	25	2,924,238	233,939	3,158,177
26	40,000	2,366,255	141,975	2,508,231	26	3,198,177	255,854	3,454,031
27	40,000	2,548,231	152,894	2,701,124	27	3,494,031	279,522	3,773,553
28	40,000	2,741,124	164,467	2,905,592	28	3,813,553	305,084	4,118,637
29	40,000	2,945,592	176,736	3,122,327	29	4,158,637	332,691	4,491,328
30	40,000	3,162,327	189,740	3,352,067	30	4,531,328	362,506	4,893,835
31	40,000	3,392,067	203,524	3,595,591	31	4,933,835	394,707	5,328,541
32	40,000	3,635,591	218,135	3,853,727	32	5,368,541	429,483	5,798,025
33	40,000	3,893,727	233,624	4,127,350	33	5,838,025	467,042	6,305,067
34	40,000	4,167,350	250,041	4,417,391	34	6,345,067	507,605	6,852,672
35	40,000	4,457,391	267,443	4,724,835	35	6,892,672	551,414	7,444,086

CHAPTER 7

Barriers to Saving and Understanding Debt

For the *Time and Money* game plan to work and for you to reach economic freedom, you have to let go of the self-defeating cultural context that convinces you that you can never save. The new money story and goals you wrote for Chapter 5 set the vision for a different relationship to debt and saving. Chapter 6 showed you the incredible power of geometric progression. In this chapter, we'll explore some basic approaches to saving so you can gather and store the fuel that will unleash the power of geometric progression to work on your behalf, and we'll also look at the negative effects of compound interest on debt.

Barriers to Saving

Mahatma Gandhi proved that we could live on the equivalent of three bowls of rice a day. It doesn't take much to sustain us. In the game plan I outline in this book, I ask you to move toward saving at least 20 percent of what you earn. The idea of saving 20 percent of what we earn can be very hard to accept because of our cultural imprints. I used to teach the children of my clients the principle of spending less than they made, and I showed them charts to demonstrate that they would be economically free by their thirties or forties if they followed this plan. They got it right away. It is really quite simple: spend less than you make, or make more than you spend. From this date forth, set a game plan to spend no more than 80 percent of what you make.

Some people say they need all of the money they make to live on now. They say there is simply no excess for saving. When people tell me they cannot save for retirement because they need to live on all their money, I start wondering what they plan to live on when they retire and are no longer making any money! Relying on Social Security alone would most likely entail living a severely diminished lifestyle.

As the years go by, we rarely notice our increases in spending and our tendency to spend whatever we make. It's worth considering the times in our lives when we had no choice but to be frugal. When I was going to college, I had to scrape together every nickel, and I worked during the summers. I searched for bargains everywhere I went. If I wanted to read a magazine, I would go to the store and read magazines off the shelf and then, to maintain a good relationship with the proprietors, I would buy just one. I would be very careful in choosing any book I decided to buy, because a book was a big purchase for me at the time.

One of the greatest bargains I found in those days was an offer in *Outdoor Life* for a whole package of Gillette Red Blades for $2.95. I had been using the more expensive Blue Blades, but at $2.95, I ordered the Red Blades. They even came in a red package. It turned out to be an appropriate color! When I shaved with them, it was like shaving backward with a butter knife. The more I shaved with them, the sharper the blades got. I used Red Blades all through college.

When I graduated from law school, I got my first job working for a year for the State Supreme Court. Then I started working at a law office, where I was paid $450 a month. With my increased income, my spending automatically went up. I started to buy a little better soap, better razor blades, and softer toilet paper. I have found that there is plenty of discretionary spending, even for the staples. My story is pretty typical of most people's. As our income goes up, we spend more and more. We think that we deserve it, that we've earned it, that we need to compensate ourselves for working so hard.

It is part of our cultural imprint to spend all we make and never save. Yet if we're honest with ourselves, we have to admit we lived very well before the last three pay raises, which we could have been putting into our savings. When a couple marries, it would be very simple to save 70 percent of one salary. When couples have their first child, most of them still do fine even though they typically lose one salary and have another mouth to feed. I knew a dentist whose wife was a hygienist whose work supported them while he went through dental school. After he graduated, they continued to live on her income and saved his salary. In seven years, they were financially free and could live their dreams both personally and professionally.

We are a nation of natural spenders, not natural savers. The cultural endorsement of spending rather than saving makes it hard to be a great saver. No matter how much they earn, I guarantee you that most people are broke at the end of the month. But if you save 20 percent of what you earn each month through automatic payroll deductions and invest it in a safe environment, you will still be broke at the end of the month. The only difference is that you will have saved 20 percent of your income, setting you well on your way to economic freedom! The key is to make this a habit.

Very few people save money, but without exception all good savers believe that they have no choice. If they don't reduce debt or save money, they become very anxious. They have discovered what they need to be happy, and they stop spending money on anything else. Before he died, Sam Walton had an estimated net worth of over $22 billion, and every day he wore the same faded jeans and a white cowboy shirt and drove a 1970 Ford F100 pickup truck. He discovered early the secret of what made him happy.

The reasons for not saving are both behavioral and procedural. The procedural component concerns the specific numbers, such as how much we save or spend each month or where it makes sense to invest our money. Writing out goals and following the specific steps in the *Time and Money* game plan are procedural components. In our attempt to accumulate money, the behavioral component is the most important and the most difficult to change because human behavior is emotionally based and intellectually rationalized. When we're dealing with behavioral issues, we don't do what we know we would be wise to do. These behavioral patterns stem from the cultural and family imprints that we discussed in Chapter 4. Learn to spot your behavioral patterns and acknowledge them to someone else. Talk to your partner about your negative behavioral patterns so that he or she can bring them to your attention when you backslide. Then you can stop yourself. Once we recognize and identify the behaviors that prevent us from saving, we can stop the behavior and start saving. Developing a new context for saving, writing a new life story, and writing down specific saving goals will help break these behavioral patterns.

Some people think that if they refinance their loans, their monthly payments will be enough lower that they can start saving money. While I have never seen people successfully borrow themselves out of debt, sometimes refinancing changes their financial structure in such a way that it allows them to become savers. Once you start saving, eventually you become a saver. You re-create your identity and come to see yourself as a saver instead of a spender or a borrower. If you refinance your house to consolidate your loans, be very careful. It takes great discipline to make sure that you don't simply take on new debt. I do not recommend debt consolidation loans because there are substantial loan application fees that usually mean you don't really save anything in interest, and you set the interest clock back at the beginning. Another problem arises if you pay off your credit cards but over the next few months again spend up to the credit limits. Now you have a large loan or second mortgage on your house, and in six to eight months all of your credit lines are up to their limits, and you've only made the situation worse.

If you decide to consolidate your debt, you absolutely have to stop spending. You have to stop using your credit cards for at least six months to ensure that you have received the cure. Get rid of all your credit cards and close all your lines of credit. Be sure you are committed to not returning to old habits. The repayment period that you select needs to reflect the useful life of the assets you are refinancing. If you take out a fifteen-year or a thirty-year mortgage to pay off assets that will be obsolete in five years, you will be making payments and paying interest on assets that you no longer have. Make a commitment today never to borrow money again. The only exception might be buying a house or paying for further education. If you pay cash for things, you never need credit.

If you are living a lavish lifestyle that uses up all your money, there is no way you can save. The problem may be that your country club peer group has a certain lifestyle that you cannot afford. Your choices are to acknowledge either that you do not belong in this setting or that you need to make more money. This may mean taking on another job or improving the efficiency of your business if you're an owner. Remember, when it is difficult to save, we try to get a higher return on our money, leaving us prey to get-rich-quick schemes. With the right business coaching, most people can make more money in their own business. Give yourself a time limit to increase your income. If in one or two years you are not making more money, then change your lifestyle by getting rid of your country club home and moving into something that you can truly afford.

Some people need to acknowledge that they are not good at saving. For these people, I recommend forced savings, which are investment vehicles that tie you in, such as pension plans or whole life insurance policies. These programs work because we are creatures of habit. Returns are not generally as good in forced savings, but at least you're able to preserve the principal and earn some interest. If the principal gets big enough, it won't really matter that you missed out on higher interest. This is one of the few circumstances in which I would recommend a pension plan for an owner of a business (see Chapter 11) or a whole life insurance policy for an individual (see Chapter 15).

The best approach to savings is to pay yourself first by automatically withdrawing a set amount of money from your bank or payroll each month and depositing it into the bank account or money market account that you have set up to fund tax-free municipal bonds or long-term CDs. It is better to have a smaller percentage of interest on something that is going into savings than a larger amount of interest on nothing.

Greg Stanley's set of tapes entitled *The Twenty-Five Real Reasons Why You Don't Save Money* (see Appendix I) extensively reviews the behaviors that prevent people from saving and outlines some basic strategies to transform them into savers.

Understanding Debt

Debt keeps us imprisoned and prevents us from living lives of freedom and independence. Being overburdened with financial responsibilities increases our stress and can even destroy what could have been great relationships. By changing our spending and saving habits one step at a time, we can regain control of our lives. Here I will give you an idea of what interest payments really cost us and what we need to do to change our spending habits. In John M. Cummuta's excellent set of tapes entitled *Turn Your Debt into Wealth* (see Appendix I), he states, "Every time you make a purchase on credit, you need to consider not just the price you're paying for the product, but the price plus interest plus how much that money could have earned as an investment."

Average Americans today have seven credit cards and pay about 92 percent of their monthly disposable income on debt payments. We have spent tomorrow's money already and are making payments on it. According to the latest U.S. Census, the average family's collective balance on all credit cards is over $8,000. If this family makes just the minimum payment, it would take them 37.5 years to pay off the balance; over that time, they will make a total payment of over $21,000, of which $13,000 is interest. This is just as if someone were to say to you: "I will lend you $8,000, and you will pay me back $21,000." If you were to invest the $13,000 in an IRA account, it would grow to $130,815 over thirty years at 8 percent interest.

You may think this does not apply to you because you have a credit card with a guaranteed 5 percent interest rate. However, if you are late or miss one payment, the interest rate could jump to 20 percent or more and last the duration of your loan. Any time you are late with a payment and are charged a late fee, call the credit card company and dispute the charges because of postal delays or extenuating circumstances. Most of the time, these charges will be dropped and will not appear on your credit report.

Each purchase that you finance costs you the price plus interest; to figure out what this comes to, multiply your monthly payment by the number of months of the loan (for example, forty-eight months). As an example, a $25,000 car might really cost you $29,000 because of the $4,000 you'd be paying in interest. If instead you put that $4,000 into your IRA account, it could grow to $40,250 over thirty years at 8 percent interest. If you add that $40,250 to the $29,000 price of the car, you're really paying $69,250 for a $25,000 car!

With each debt, the interest you pay puts you on the wrong side of the power of the compound interest equation. It's important to realize that there is a finite amount of money you are going to make in your life. If you give too much of it away in interest payments and impulse buying, there will not be enough money left over for you to retire comfortably. There are two basic approaches you can take with your money: you can spend it on things that don't add meaning to your life and stay in debt, or you can build your financial future and retire early and in style. Every dollar you consume now brings you one dollar of value, but every dollar you invest for your future can bring you five to twenty times that amount in your retirement years, allowing you to retire ten to twenty years earlier. Reducing spending and paying off debt will eliminate your money problems and improve your relationships. It will also improve your health by reducing stress. And it will serve as a shining example for your children about what is possible.

How would it feel to be out of debt and to own your home free and clear, with utilities, taxes, and food as your only real expenses? This is possible for everyone. If they're following a clear game plan, most people can pay off all of their credit card debt in one year and their car in the second year. By the third year, they're making extra payments toward their mortgage. By the seventh to ninth year, they can be totally debt free.

When you become debt free there is no need to worry about your credit because you pay cash for all your purchases. Our ability to obtain credit is what got us into trouble in the first place. The idea that we need to build up our credit by borrowing is an illusion that keeps us in debt.

As you contemplate your particular circumstances, remember to write your financial goals down in your Time and Money Journal and on three-by-five cards. Use the chart in Appendix C to help you develop ways to increase your savings, freeing up money to pay off your debts. Once you're on the path toward saving money, follow the *Time and Money* game plan in Chapter 8 to get completely out of debt. In Chapter 8, I will also outline the other key elements of the game plan to help you harness the power of your savings and set you firmly on the road to economic freedom.

The Time and Money Game Plan for Economic Freedom

Now that you have a new money story, clearly stated goals, and a basic understanding of geometric progression, the downside of debt, and the importance of saving, coming up with a reliable game plan for economic freedom is easy.

The *Time and Money* game plan is very basic. First, write your new money story and set your goals for increasing your income, reducing your debt, and increasing your savings. Do something that you love and that is profitable, and do more of it. Take part of your money and store it in safe, liquid assets with geometric progression. Then spend the rest of your money on things that add meaning to your life. This leads to economic freedom and a life of self-integrity and peace.

Many people strive to become economically free. But in the United States, the wealthiest nation in the world, at age sixty-five only 3 percent of the population does not rely on the government or another outside source of income to survive; the vast majority do not reach economic freedom by retirement. Remember, economic freedom is the day that the interest from your safe, liquid investments reproduces the income needed to sustain your current lifestyle.

Many financial advisors give you a high dollar goal to achieve to become economically free; as I pointed out in Chapter 6, this amount is way beyond the minimum needed to live in peace with your money. Because I am debt free and well past economic freedom, I spend everything I make with absolutely no anxiety. By definition, this means that I will be able to leave my heirs the liquid assets whose interest has been providing my income. As I mentioned earlier, if you are willing to spend your liquid assets as well as your interest income, you do not have to acquire as many assets to be financially free, because your plan would include the possibility of spending almost everything before you die. Following this concept reduces the stress of striving to obtain a high economic goal earlier in your life. Economic freedom is a state of mind, which you can achieve following a safe, predictable game plan that provides you with all the money you need to live a full life. Once your game plan is in place, you can live your life as if you have already reached economic freedom. There's no further need for worry, and there's no need for hope, because once this plan is reliably set in motion, the result is a given.

When you have the proper context about money and have set in motion a game plan that works, you will have all the money you need, and money will no longer control you. Only two things can interfere with this plan: if you become disabled, or if you die. To protect yourself and your family from these disasters, you may want to consider getting disability insurance and some cheap term life insurance. I'll be discussing insurance in more detail in Chapter 15.

Developing Your Game Plan

As I've said before, culturally we've been taught to spend our income and go into debt no matter what our income. If we cannot see what is making this happen, there is no way to free ourselves from economic stress. Our habits around money are often rooted in our fear of rejection and our worries about what other people will think and say. These concerns usually stem from our poor self-acceptance, often based on childhood experiences. As we saw in

Chapter 4, it's possible to look deeply at the origins of these messages and begin to transcend them. Once we've learned to accept and be at peace with who we are, we no longer worry about what other people think or say. Then we are able to go through the step-by-step process of becoming financially free, which requires a two-pronged approach of eliminating debt and saving aggressively.

Eliminating Debt and Starting to Save

If you are in debt, eliminating that debt is a crucial first step in following the *Time and Money* game plan.

The only debt that is reasonable to incur is for the purchase of very large items such as your house, your education, or your car. Never go into debt for anything else, especially not for consumable items. I can't state it more clearly: consumption debt is bad, bad, bad, and bad! The best game plan is to spend less than you make and to save a substantial amount of your money. Then you can consume with saved dollars. Most families in America are imprinted to use their credit cards and consume whether they have the money to pay for something or not. If you do this, you typically pay high interest rates; this is not an effective way to manage your money. If you were to pay only the minimum monthly payment on a typical credit card with a 19.8 percent interest rate, it would take you thirty-one years to pay off a $2,000 balance! I recommend you cut up all your credit cards and close your accounts. You may keep one credit card for emergencies as long as you pay it off each month.

Setting a Savings Plan in Motion

To come up with an effective strategy for eliminating debt, it's important to have a clear sense of your monthly expenses (see Appendix C: Income and Expense Categories Chart) and determine how many of these expenses are payments on specific debts. Personal finance software programs such as Quicken or Microsoft Money can help you greatly in organizing this information on your computer. Start a weekly savings plan today and set an initial goal of putting away $50 a week. You can arrange to have this deducted automatically from your payroll and deposited into a special savings account at your bank that you use for debt reduction. Increase your income, and cut your spending. Begin today, and make a commitment to save now. Start putting something away, even if it's only $10 a week. I can't repeat often enough that the key to economic freedom is spending less than you make or making more than you spend. Increase the amount of money you're saving each week, with a goal of saving 20 percent of your weekly income by the end of the year to pay off debt. It's important to treat savings as an expense and pay yourself first. Most who earn $30,000 a year can find an additional $200 per month for debt reduction. Most who earn $100,000 a year can find an additional $700 per month, and most who earn $250,000 can find an additional $2,000 per month.

Save unexpected extra money, such as tax returns, bonuses, and pay raises, and immediately use this "found money" to pay off your consumer debt. Set up an automatic savings and investment plan. Look for and find areas in your expenses that you can reduce. Don't buy new cars. You can save thousands of dollars by buying a car that is a year or two old. You may want to consider taking a second job for a short period of time to help eliminate credit card debt. Some couples live on one salary and invest the other. Living life is found in the experience and the detail, and not in the number of possessions we own. We need less to live on when we move from a materialistic life to one that is more spiritual.

Once you've made a commitment toward economic freedom and debt reduction, it's important to take action by freeing up money from unnecessary expenditures. Keep track each month of where you're spending your money. Change your spending habits, and only use cash or checks to buy things.

Give yourself a set amount to spend each month, so that you get the feeling of what this is like. As an experiment, don't do any shopping for one month except for food. You may go through an initial withdrawal period. Facing your fears of rejection will help you to become wealthy. The way to stop salespeople from trying to sell you something is to simply say, "I can't afford that." If they persist, just repeat your answer. While you're reducing expenditures, be sure not to make any major purchases, such as a new car, boat, or house.

The Time and Money Game Plan

Identify your debts and place them on the Time and Money Game Plan Worksheet in Appendix E. First pay back all past-due obligations, such as back taxes. Next rank all small debts (under $10,000) by number, from the smallest amount to the largest. This category includes credit card debt, consumer debt, auto loan balances, and small student loans. Start with the smallest debt (no matter how high or low the interest), and use the money from your debt reduction savings account to pay it off first while continuing to make the minimum payments on your other debts. At the beginning, it's important to get momentum and see that you are making progress, so don't worry about the respective interest rates at the moment. If the high credit card interest rate on a larger debt bothers you, you can always call the company and negotiate a lower rate, or transfer your balance to another credit card company with a lower rate. Once you have paid off the first debt, you'll feel a sense of empowerment. Paying off that debt frees up additional money, which adds to your increased savings. Use this increased savings to pay down the next smallest debt. Fill out the worksheet in Appendix E in pencil so that you can update it each month. This will help you keep on track and stay motivated.

As you pay down debt, you gain momentum and free up more money to pay off the next debt. The money that pays off these debts comes from increased income, reduced spending, and the extra money that becomes available as you pay off each debt. If you have money saved at the outset of setting the *Time and Money* game plan into motion, for the sake of your peace of mind do *not* use it for early debt retirement for at least six months.

If you have an emergency during this time—for example, major car repairs or unexpected medical bills—you can skip a month or two of debt reduction and use the cash that would have been going towards your debts to cover the emergency. The same is true if you feel you need a vacation: skip a month or two of debt reduction and pay for your vacation with cash. Just be sure to get back on track with your debt reduction plan as soon as you can.

Once you've made progress paying down your small debt, be sure to fund your Roth IRA and any pension plan at work up to the limit where the company matches your money.

Once you've paid off all of your small debts (under $10,000), celebrate! Now take the "found money" you have freed up and use it to pay off large debts (over $10,000), such as your car loan, your home mortgage, and any lines of credit. Once you have paid off your large debt, if interest rates on tax-free municipal bonds are between 5.5 percent and 7 percent, use 50 percent of your fund to pay down long-term debt, such as business loans and large student loans (over $10,000), and the other 50 percent to add to your personal savings, which you'll be investing in tax-free municipal bonds. If interest rates are low (under 5.5 percent), use your new monthly savings and found money to pay down debt. If interest rates are high (above 7 percent), then put one-third toward paying off debt and invest the other two-thirds in tax-free municipal bonds. After you have paid off all of your long-term debts, 100 percent of your money will go into your personal savings, invested in tax-free municipal bonds (see Chapter 12).

This may seem like a slow process, but once you've paid off your basic debts and are regularly investing in your retirement funds, you'll have a considerable amount of excess money left each month to invest in tax-free municipal bonds and pay off any long-term debts. By following the *Time and Money* game plan, most people can pay off all their credit card debt in one year and their car in the second year. By the third year, they are making extra payments toward their mortgage. Most people following this plan can be debt free and pay off their home in five to nine years (see Chapter 14).

Once you pay off your home, about 40 percent of your income will be available to invest in your savings. This will allow you to become totally financially free in another eight or nine years, as we discussed in Chapter 6.

The following diagram illustrates the different phases of the *Time and Money* game plan. Do Exercise 6 in Appendix A, and use the worksheet in Appendix E to identify the specific steps in your personal game plan. As a review, Appendix G contains a summary of the *Time and Money* game plan.

Time and Money Game Plan Diagram

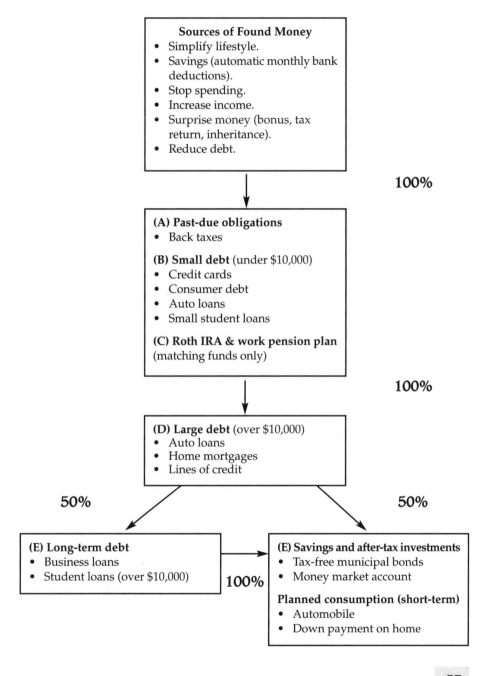

Sources of Found Money
- Simplify lifestyle.
- Savings (automatic monthly bank deductions).
- Stop spending.
- Increase income.
- Surprise money (bonus, tax return, inheritance).
- Reduce debt.

100%

(A) Past-due obligations
- Back taxes

(B) Small debt (under $10,000)
- Credit cards
- Consumer debt
- Auto loans
- Small student loans

(C) Roth IRA & work pension plan (matching funds only)

100%

(D) Large debt (over $10,000)
- Auto loans
- Home mortgages
- Lines of credit

50%

50%

(E) Long-term debt
- Business loans
- Student loans (over $10,000)

100%

(E) Savings and after-tax investments
- Tax-free municipal bonds
- Money market account

Planned consumption (short-term)
- Automobile
- Down payment on home

The Ten Principles of Investment and Debt

By following these ten principles, you can achieve economic freedom:

1. The key to economic freedom is to make more than you spend, or spend less than you make.
2. Make sure that every asset, large and small, adds meaning to your life.
3. Your best source of money is your ability to earn it, not investing.
4. If you have it made, don't risk it. You now have the ability to save enough money to retire early if you just play it smart by putting your money in safe investments where you do not lose your principal and where you earn a specific rate of return.
5. Since your source of money is your ability to earn it, not investing, focus on ways to increase your income, improve your efficiency, and earn more.
6. No matter how much you make, always save some. It is important to begin saving, no matter how much. Spend less than you make, or make more than you spend.
7. Except for material possessions that add meaning to your life, keep all savings in liquid assets.
8. Insurance is not an investment according to these principles. Its only purpose is to replace money in the case of an unacceptable loss, such as disability or death; keep it to the minimum necessary. Once you reach economic freedom, it is an unnecessary expenditure.
9. Purchasing a home is an effective use of debt. Although it is not a liquid asset, it adds meaning to your life. Homes have also proven to be a good long-term investment and provide a hedge against inflation.
10. Debt:
    a. Always save for consumption; never borrow (for consumer items, vacations, and so forth).
    b. Cut up all credit cards except one for emergencies and pay off that credit card and any other consumer debt in full each month.
    c. Create a plan to pay off your house (when returns on liquid investments are low, accelerate your house payments).

CHAPTER 9

Fundamental Principles of the Time and Money Game Plan

When I first started my practice as a financial consultant, I knew economic freedom was important. I also knew that people could achieve economic freedom fairly easily. I had grand dreams about how I could make a big difference in people's lives. I developed great retirement plans where they could accumulate gigantic amounts of money. I prepared wonderfully clear documents and charts showing my clients the sure path to economic freedom. I had the illusion that in this way I could help my clients commit themselves to a safe economic game plan and change their lives.

I soon became discouraged because many of my clients and their advisors turned around and made a mess out of my finely designed plans. They would take money out of their retirement plans to buy art objects, Buick Rivieras, wasteful and unnecessary life insurance policies, risky stocks, and speculative real estate. And the many losses in their investment portfolios prevented geometric progression of their retirement plan, undermining my advice.

Many of my clients asked me what I knew about investing, and I tried to show them mathematically so they could see the possibilities when principal is never lost. The kind of investment that would fit my generic description back then was only producing 5 or 6 percent. I remember telling a neurosurgeon to put his money in a safe, reliable investment paying a 5 to 6 percent return, but he wanted something that was paying 20 percent. So I devised a structure to show him that by the end of fifteen years, if he followed my plan, he would be economically free. There is always the possibility that we could do better or worse in the stock market, but if we have it made, why risk it? We seem to have an infinite capacity to stress ourselves, especially when it comes to money. To a large degree, this comes from greed and ego. It often seems that the more money we make, the more we stress ourselves. The neurosurgeon did not like the safe but boring program I recommended, so he selected a stressful path and placed his money in the stock market.

Over time, I got better at explaining the game plan, and so more people decided to follow my advice. After ten or twelve years of investing this way, my clients would say to me, "I'm doing way better with my pension plan, even with your boring program!" A steady geometric progression with no leaks always gets the best results.

Let me tell you another story. When I first began practicing law, I met a doctor named Bob and we became very close friends. Because we were friends and he heard about what I was doing, he asked me if I would give him advice about his pension plan. So I helped him set up a game plan. He was a really good producer, but he had not accumulated many assets because he had invested in the stock market, and occasionally in gold and silver. He had even tried commodities. He was an extremely bright fellow, but he hadn't gained much ground with his investments, though he seemed to enjoy the fun of playing the market.

I asked Bob to trust me and to follow the safe, boring context in my game plan, which will invariably lead to a geometric progression that yields a massive result. Most clients can be economically free in a relatively short time if they follow this advice. My normal practice was to write such a recommendation down on a piece of paper and have my clients give it to their brokers.

A year after I had given Bob his plan, he came in for the annual meeting we had agreed upon. I found out that Bob had not followed my recommendations. He had invested in something else, and it was down a little. He had not even achieved the first fold of the metaphorical tissue paper, and he was already going backward. I talked to him for another half hour about the wisdom of the program I was recommending. He smiled and said, "Yes, of course," but at our next annual meeting he had ignored my advice again and slipped even further behind. The third year he was up a little, but still down on geometric progression. Each year when we met, I tried to increase the tempo of my speech to make it more enchanting, but by the time we had reached the seventh year, he was down about one-third from my program. He just never seemed to be able to follow my advice to the letter.

The eighth year when he came in, Bob was extremely happy. I was absolutely thrilled when he showed me his portfolio. If he had sold his investments at that moment, he would have been a year and a half ahead of where he would have been if he had followed my program. He had invested in gold and silver futures, and they were nearing their peak. I went around the desk, gave him a big hug, and said, "That's terrific, Bob! Now it's time to sell and put your portfolio in a safe environment." I gave him a two-hour lecture about all of the good and the bad things I had seen over the years. I gave him the paper about where to invest, and he walked out.

About two months later, I was having lunch and ran into Bob. "Boy, you really got out of that in time," I remarked. I knew that two weeks after our last meeting, the scandal had come out about the Hunt brothers trying to corner the silver market, and gold and silver futures had dropped like rocks. But Bob looked anything but happy. It seemed he hadn't followed my advice, and instead had lost about 70 percent of what he had. Bob is still not doing what I advocate. If he had followed what I had said, he would have been four times past economic freedom by now. Economic freedom for him was $300,000 a year for the rest of his life without touching the principal. After his loss in gold and silver futures, Bob continued to do what he had done, and he eventually quit coming to see me about five years ago. He was simply unwilling to change his mind because he kept looking at his losses and was always hoping that he'd somehow regain the fortune he'd lost by doing things his way. Bob's story exemplifies the importance of never taking unnecessary risks.

I teach from my life experiences. Over the years, I have tried just about everything, especially with regard to money. The things that didn't work, I don't teach. I once went bankrupt because I tried something that did not work. I started over again from nothing, and using a solid game plan I became financially free and completely out of debt within ten years. I have now accumulated enough liquid assets compounding in a safe environment that if I wanted to quit working at this moment, I could do so and continue to live in the style to which I have become accustomed. From my many life experiences and my work as a financial mentor for over forty years, I have developed a consistent philosophy and a game plan of investing that can work for anyone.

Economic Strategies

In my money context, I want to reach economic freedom as safely and quickly as I can. People have a wide range of economic strategies. Some diffuse their money by placing it into a wide range of investments such as real estate, stocks, and limited partnerships, hoping that one will strike it rich. This strategy is not efficient or reliable. Another strategy some people use is to reduce the amount of taxes they pay. Personally, I know that the more taxes I pay, the more money I am making. Americans have a history of hating taxes. One of the things that pushed us into the American Revolution was taxation by England without representation. So it's not surprising that one popular economic program revolves around avoiding taxes. In the 1970s and 1980s, there were tax shelters that were really taxes in disguise. Some people are so busy avoiding taxes that they lose sight of the goal of economic freedom. Some people actually buy larger houses than they need so that they'll have a larger amount of interest they can write off on their taxes! The problem is that they're still losing the interest they cannot write off. Saving money on taxes is inappropriate if it costs more money than it saves.

Focus instead on your vision and the *Time and Money* game plan of saving and debt reduction, which will lead you inevitably toward economic freedom. Everyone in this country could become financially free if they spent less than they made or made more than they spent and invested the difference in safe, liquid assets.

Four Basic Criteria for Selecting Investments

Instead of recommending specific investments, I have come up with four criteria to help clients make the best possible investments based on the market and their level of risk tolerance. The most important rule in this basic generic description is: *Safety first!* After the plan is set reliably in motion, the other three criteria are to choose assets that show no loss of principal, that are always compounding, and that maximize your tax deferral. I then select an investment that meets these criteria while giving the highest rate of return at that time. The investments that currently meet this generic description for your retirement environment (that is, your pension or Roth IRA) are U.S. government treasuries (bonds, notes, and bills), government agency bonds, bank certificates of deposit (CDs), and money market accounts. For personal (after-tax) investments, I recommend AAA-rated general obligation municipal bonds. I'll be describing each of these investment vehicles in greater depth in Chapter 12.

If an investment contradicts even one of my four basic criteria, I don't recommend it. Following these principles dramatically limits where you can invest. There are only about ten kinds of investments that meet all four guidelines. Out of these choices, I have my broker look around the country for the highest rate of return.

We first need to set up and stick to a consistent game plan that allows us enough money to place in a safe environment that will never lose the principal and that will grow and compound every year. Remember the example of the tissue paper in Chapter 6? Anything we do at the beginning is magnified exponentially at the end when geometric progression is working for us. In order of priority, safety is first, then setting the game plan reliably in motion with consistent compounding. Following these principles and this definition of safety, the investment will be able to survive an economic depression as bad as the one in 1929. It's not worth getting 2 percent more and exposing yourself to greater risk.

If You Have It Made, Don't Risk It

The safety first rule in my generic criteria means that if you have it made, don't risk it. Anyone reading this book has the ability to save a percentage of what they make to pay off debt and to invest in liquid assets. As you can see from the charts in Chapter 6, you can invest in safe and liquid assets and have all you need to live in economic peace. Taking a higher risk to get a bit higher interest rate can significantly increase your level of stress. We all remember what happened to investments in the years 2000 and 2001, after so many people had traded safety for risk. Many people thought that index mutual funds were very safe and would never lose principal. According to the *Time and Money* definition of safety, a good investment is one that would survive a Great Depression like the one that began in 1929, the worst economic conditions in American history, and never lose principal. Investment vehicles that meet this generic description include United States treasury notes and bonds, government agency bonds, bank certificates of deposit (CDs) for pension plans, IRAs, and other tax-deferred environments. For your personal investment environment (the money you're investing that you've already paid taxes on), I would recommend money market accounts and general obligation tax-free municipal bonds with underlying ratings of AAA. In the economy of the early twenty-first century, I would not recommend corporate bonds. If treasury notes and bank CDs meet the generic description of safety, I select the CD with the highest rate of return. There may be a 2 percent spread in interest between treasury bills and time CDs and government agency bonds. Remember, the initial small difference in interest makes a huge difference at the end, so within the definition of safety, be sure to choose the highest rate of return.

BEST INVESTMENTS FOR TAX-DEFERRED AND AFTER-TAX INCOME

INVESTMENT ENVIRONMENT	TAX-DEFERRED (PENSIONS, 401(K), IRAS)	PERSONAL AFTER-TAX
Investment type	• U.S. treasury notes and bonds • Zero-coupon treasury bonds • Government agency bonds • Bank certificates of deposit (CDs)	• AAA-rated tax-free general obligation municipal bonds • Money market accounts

Once a client told me, "Consistent with your generic criteria, I can get government-insured time CDs with an 18 percent return." I asked him where, and he replied, "Israel." Wherever there is high inflation, there are high interest rates. Of course, we're all familiar with the uncertainty in the Middle East.

In my personal nonretirement, after-tax financial environment, I prefer tax-free municipal bonds. One client asked me about Philippine bonds that were paying twice what U.S. bonds were paying. We went into a discussion about safety in the Philippines. If you're getting a high interest rate, you are taking a risk. If your brother-in-law says that he will pay you 20 percent on a loan, you're clearly taking a high risk, because if your brother-in-law could get a lower interest rate from a bank he would take it. And the bank expects him to pay the money back!

Yield Curves

The yield curves for bonds, CDs, and treasuries change as returns (yields) go up or down. I recommend that you buy bonds with maturities where the curve starts to flatten out (the point where increases in interest rates become minimal), which in 2004 is somewhere around year nine on tax-free municipal bonds.

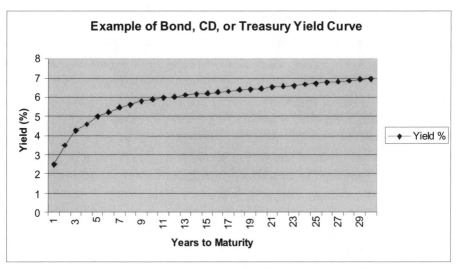

Example of yield curve for treasuries, bonds, and CDs (note that the line in this example starts flattening at ten years). This yield curve graph is an example only and does not necessarily reflect current yields.

In the past, bond yield curves flattened at around ten to fifteen years. The longer it is until a bond's maturity, the greater the risk you are taking. If you buy a $10,000 ten-year bond, you might get a return of 6 percent. By going out another twenty years, you might get a slightly better rate, but not that much better; for a thirty-year bond, you'd possibly get 6.2 percent instead of 6 percent, but your risk would increase significantly. For example, if interest rates increased 2 percent and you needed to sell your bond early, you might get $8,500 for a ten-year $10,000 bond, but the resell value of the thirty-year bond might be as low as $4,500. I recommend that you stay within the five-year to fifteen-year range. When you keep your bond to maturity, you always get back the face value of the bond no matter what the interest rate is at that time. Each year, as you invest in bonds that mature where the yield curve flattens, you will automatically be laddering your bonds; this means that each year you will have bonds maturing. In this way, you will always have money from your maturing bonds that can be used either to reinvest in potentially higher yielding bonds or to pay for needed expenses. You won't want to invest in long-term bonds if it is likely that you will need the money soon, for example to buy a house or to pay for your children's college educations.

Importance of Investing in Your Personal Financial Environment

Once you have funded your Roth IRA and pension plan (to the point where funds are matched), you can then fund your personal investment environment to get to the goal line of economic freedom faster. Matched money is important because it is free money from your employer and is like getting a 100 percent return on your investment. Little differences in your personal financial environment make gigantic differences in how fast you can get to economic freedom. When you retire, you first use the money in your personal financial environment (tax-free municipal bonds), which allows your retirement plan to keep growing in the most efficient way.

If you are in the highest tax bracket, the best investment would be AAA-rated tax-free municipal bonds. Fewer than 5 percent of my clients who have invested in both their personal and retirement financial environments even use their retirement funds until they have reached the age where the government requires them to withdraw from their accounts.

Gambling Fund

Many of my clients have told me that what I teach is boring, but when they start to see the long-term results, it starts to get exciting. My observations over the years lead me to believe that human beings find gambling innately appealing. Because many of us seem to need the thrill and excitement of gambling, what I now recommend is that people set money aside for a gambling fund if this kind of excitement is meaningful to them.

The important thing is not to confuse gambling with investing. When we get really clear about the fact that we love to see things go up and down and this adds fun to our lives, then it makes sense to take the risk with a set amount that doesn't threaten our retirement savings or our personal savings. Having a gambling fund can help add spice to contrast the otherwise boring and safe program I am recommending. For example, once you have set your *Time and Money* game plan reliably in motion, you may want to invest $10,000 in the stock market. You might choose to invest in individual stocks or in mutual funds. That way, when you come home and open the newspaper, you can tell whether to be happy or sad! When we don't set small amounts of money aside for gambling, too often we're tempted to gamble with our retirement money. We can find dozens of ways to rationalize these choices, but the bottom line is this: some like to gamble slowly in the stock market or real estate, while others like to go to Vegas and mainline.

I often say that I have made twenty-eight thousand mistakes in my life, but fortunately I rarely repeat any one mistake. During my life, one thing I had not done was to invest in commodities. My clients were always asking me about commodities, but I had no direct experience with them. I felt if I were going to teach people not to invest in commodities, it would be worthwhile to have at least a bit of experience with them. It turned out to be one of the shortest experiences I've ever had. I found the best commodity broker in Chicago and gave him $10,000 to invest. He recommended investing in potatoes and gave me plenty of seemingly good reasons. Within one week, he lost $5,000 because we were highly leveraged. I took the other $5,000 back, and I personally invested in corn the next week and lost it all. It was more fun for me to lose it than for my broker to lose it! And that is my total life experience in commodities.

Because we soon see how erratic the results are with our gambling fund, such experiments help reinforce our commitment to the conservative *Time and Money* game plan. Sometimes we do get ahead with our gambling fund. This is great, but it is not the way to remove stress from our economic lives or to reach economic peace of mind. Sometimes I'm surprised at clients who have stayed on track for many years in this program and who then take chances with their portfolios. One of my very first clients, who was already way beyond economic freedom, called me to tell me he had invested one-third of his portfolio in the stock market. He said he had met someone on an airplane who was president of an up-and-coming company, and he had decided to invest 30 percent of his pension plan into this company. As it turned out, this was just before the 1987 crash. When the crash came, he lost 20 percent of his investment and asked me what he should do. I recommended that he sell the stock and place it back into his safe environment. I wish I had set up a gambling fund for this client at the beginning, but he looked like the last person on Earth who would gamble in this way. When I geometrically progressed out that one slip, I calculated it would cost him around $3 million in his lifetime. Never put your retirement funds at risk!

What about Inflation?

Many people wonder how inflation affects the *Time and Money* game plan. When we have inflation, interest rates go up. That is why a retirement plan with a conservative return will in the end totally outstrip inflation and even amplify your return. Many people have been told that their money will not keep up with inflation, but as I showed you in Chapter 6, this is not true in a tax-deferred or tax-free financial environment. Municipal bonds and treasury bonds routinely beat inflation by about 2 percent. Tax-free municipal bonds beat inflation by 4 to 6 percent.

Inflation is not predictable. It is transitory, and it is something that we cannot control. As I mentioned earlier, many brokers try to scare their clients with the idea that if they don't take a risk and invest in possibly higher return stocks, inflation will take away all their profits. This is not true. Two things happen as inflation increases: first, your salary or your prices or fees also go up. As you make a higher salary and follow the *Time and Money* game plan, you put more into your investments with geometric progression. Second, during inflation interest rates also go up, and you get a bigger return on your investments. A tax-deferred compounding geometric progression will always outperform inflation. Inflation adds fuel to geometric progression, and you get incredible results.

Sticking with the Basic Principles

The *Time and Money* strategy employs a fairly simple game plan, but like a diamond it has many facets. When I first started doing this, I would tell my clients to put their money in a steady geometric progression so they would not lose it. Many wanted to put it into the stock market instead and get a higher return than the boring 5 or 6 percent return from the safer investments I was advising. If you go into the stock market and break even or lose in just one of the years, you have really lost a fortune because you'll miss out on the last metaphorical fold at the end of the geometric progression. So just by breaking even, you could lose hundreds of thousands of dollars. Over the past ten years, the stock market has gone up dramatically and the stock market has gone down dramatically. If you have two or three years of just breaking even, that alone can cost you a fortune. Steady geometric progression not only makes you the most money, it is also the safest and most reliable way to invest. In the next chapter, we'll look at some of the risks of the stock market, before going on to discuss safe and reliable investments in Chapter 11 and Chapter 12.

CHAPTER 10

Understanding the Risks of the Market

Very few people understand the stock market, and no one can accurately predict changes in the market. Many brokers tell you to buy a stock when it is high and tell you not to buy when it drops. Common sense would tell us the best time to buy stocks is when they're low. When we invest in equities (stocks) we are always on shifting sands; we are always taking a risk. When you have a game plan to obtain economic freedom that is safe and predictable, why take such a risk? Anyone who can work and save money has it made; economic freedom is yours for the taking. Your ability to earn money is the most important thing in developing economic abundance. Your income goes up in times of inflation, so you can store away even more money. Investments are for your retirement and your peace of mind, not to make you rich. Your earnings from your job will make you rich if you live within your means and consistently save or store part of them.

Economics and the market are always changing. The day we think the market is really good is typically the day just before it goes down. Investing in stocks may make you a little more money, but what is your peace of mind worth? I want to show you how to get rid of the fundamental insecurity that most of us carry around about money. During a bear market (a down or negative market), treasuries have always outperformed the stock market. With safe United States treasury securities, you don't have to worry about how stocks are doing. This peace of mind affects the way you look at life. It affects your relationship with other people.

On a theoretical basis, being in the stock market will yield better results over the long haul in a bull market (an up or positive market) than the approach I am recommending. Most investors in the stock market don't stay with a consistent strategy, and instead jump in and out of the market and get mediocre returns. They would be better off in most cases to consistently invest in index funds like the S&P or the Dow. But statistics do not help your peace of mind or give you a sense of freedom when it comes to the rough times in the stock market. With a good context of investing, when the market goes down, it just becomes interesting because your stomach is not going down with it.

No individual stock is absolutely safe on a long-term basis. In 1920 there were thirty-four major automobile manufacturers in the United States, and today there are just five. We do not know which company is going to survive, and no one can reliably predict economic ups and downs. In the Great Depression that began in 1929, General Motors went down 95 percent! The United States has experienced many minidepressions, which are called recessions. A recession is when the economy is going down, and a depression is when it is severely down.

If the stock market knew whether it was going up or down tomorrow, it would already be there, so every day it is always 50-50. The market will go down the same way it goes up. When we're experiencing the good times, we always think this time it will be different and never end. Significant drops in the stock market happened in 1929, 1966, 1973, 1987, and most recently, in March 2000—that is, at the top of every bull market. In the last two hundred-plus years of American economic history, there have been seven bull markets and seven bear markets. And every time we've had a bull market, people have thought it was going to be different and never end.

In the early part of the new millennium, we came out of the best bull market in two hundred years of American history—a bull market that thrived from 1982 to 2000 (although the market crashed in 1987, overall this period was a bull market). Michael A. Alexander, in his book *Stock Cycles* (see Appendix I), says the average bull market in American history lasted approximately fourteen years, and the average bear market lasted just under fourteen years. The duration ranged from eight years on the short side to over twenty years on the long side.

The overall return for investments during bear markets was 0.3 percent, while the overall return for investments in bull markets was 13.2 percent. This is why the S&P 500 and Dow Jones index funds do so well during bull markets and treasury securities beat the 0.3% return of index funds during bear markets. Some market analysts say that the bear market that started in March 2000 could last ten to twenty years.

The P/E (price to earnings) ratio is another indicator of how well the market is doing. The price to earnings ratio is the figure you get when you divide the price of the stock by its earnings per share. If the price of the stock is $28 and the earnings per share is $2, the price to earnings ratio would be $14 to $1, or 14. The average P/E ratio for the past sixty years has been 14. If the P/E is less than 14, the stock is considered a bargain; if the P/E is over 14, it is considered overpriced. A high P/E ratio is a cause for concern. The normal safe P/E ratio is 14, and in the year 2003 the average market P/E ratio was 35, with the S&P 500 P/E in the high 20s. At the peak of the last bull market, the P/Es were in the high 30s, and we are not that far off. During the late 1990s, some high-tech stocks were priced at 400 times their earnings! At the bottom of the last bear market, in 1982, the P/Es were somewhere between 6 and 8. Right now, we aren't even close to that.

Equities (stocks) returned an average of 7 percent a year over the roughly two hundred years from 1800 to 1998. There have been long periods in recent American history where they yielded zero or a negative return on investment, such as the twenty-five years from 1929 to 1954 and the seventeen years from 1965 to 1982. There have also been times of massive loss, such as 1987, when the market experienced the largest one-day drop in history and the average mutual fund was down 30 percent. More recently, in the years 2000 to 2002, we saw a loss of over $4 trillion in the stock market.

Stocks Are Risky

The stock market is an arena abounding with risks, some of which could result in your losing everything if you're heavily invested in equities. When there's a solid, reliable game plan that can lead you inevitably toward economic freedom, why would you want to play around with such risks?

Investing in stocks carries a much greater risk than investing in bonds, especially for the novice investor. I would not recommend putting retirement money in stocks. For those of you who enjoy the excitement and roller coaster ride of the market and need to experience taking a risk with your money, this is an ideal place for your gambling fund. But please don't risk your retirement, your children's education, or the opportunity to live out your lifestyle dreams on the roll of the dice in the stock market. Instead, place that money in a safe environment, such as tax-free municipal bonds for your personal savings, and government treasuries, notes, and bonds for your retirement plan.

If you're already heavily invested in the market, the best thing to do is the right thing at the moment, which is to sell. You may not have the stomach for this, so stay where you are and start investing the new money you save following the more conservative *Time and Money* game plan. Adopting this context will send you to bed every night sleeping like a well-contented baby because you feel abundant and safe.

CHAPTER 11

Rating Your Investments and Investing for Tax Efficiency

For all of the reasons we have discussed in earlier chapters, always fund your tax-free retirement environment first, such as a Roth IRA, and then your tax-deferred 401(k) plan at work, especially if your work plan matches the money you put in. Because these plans are in a tax-deferred or a tax-free environment, you can use U.S. treasuries (bonds, notes, or bills), government agency bonds, bank CDs (certificates of deposit), or zero-coupon government agency bonds. Once you have completely funded your tax-free and tax-deferred retirement environments, put your after-tax money into tax-free municipal bonds for your personal investment environment.

IRAs (Individual Retirement Accounts)

Individual retirement accounts (IRAs) were developed by the government to encourage people to save money for retirement. With an

IRA, the government allows you to put up to $3,000 away each year ($3,500 if you're over fifty years old) in an account where you will not be taxed on the interest earned. The maximum contribution is slated to go up to $4,000 in 2005 and then to $5,000 in 2008 for those up to fifty years old. For those over fifty years of age, the maximum contribution will be $4,500 in 2005, $5,000 in 2006, and $6,000 in the year 2008. There are two basic types of IRAs: traditional IRAs (including SEP-IRAs for self-employed earners, which generally allow larger contributions based on a percentage of income) and Roth IRAs.

All of the accumulations and compounding of earnings grow tax-free in a Roth IRA and tax-deferred in a traditional IRA. If you recall the metaphor for geometric progression we discussed in Chapter 6, you know that a little bit at the beginning of the folding process can result in a fortune by the final fold. Whatever the government doesn't take away in taxes remains to participate in the magic of geometric progression. This could result in a three times greater return on your money over thirty years than if you had placed it in a taxed environment. There is a big difference between money that is geometrically compounding in a tax-deferred or tax-free environment and money that is accumulating in a taxed environment.

Tax-Deferred Income Versus Tax-Free Income at Retirement

Tax-free municipal bonds and Roth IRAs are particularly great in that you pay no tax on the interest or principal when you withdraw it at retirement, and the government can rarely affect your return. But because the money in most retirement plans is taxed when you withdraw it, if the government changes the rules by the time you retire, the tax rate might be higher than the 15 to 33 percent bracket it is now. From 1940 to 1981, the top marginal individual federal income tax rate ranged from 70 to 94 percent. Because of the increase in the retired population, meaning there may eventually be only two people working for each retiree, additional taxes may be needed to shore up the Social Security and Medicare system. I would rather pay my taxes now and not worry about what the tax rate will be when I retire.

For this reason, I recommend the Roth IRA because it permits tax-free payout of both contributions and accumulated earnings if held for at least five years and held past the age of fifty-nine and a half, to death, or during disability. With a traditional IRA, you receive a tax deduction for the initial contribution, but you have to pay taxes when you withdraw your money at retirement. When you withdraw the money from a Roth IRA at retirement, you save up to 40 percent of the income from taxes as compared to a traditional IRA that is fully taxed.

Pension Plans for Small Businesses

In most cases I recommend *against* employers and owners of small businesses having 401(k) or pension plans unless the pension-related nonrecoverable costs (contributions to employees, money spent on management costs to accountants, actuaries, lawyers, or financial planners) can be kept to less than 10 to 12 percent of the plan's contributions. It would be better for you not to have a plan and instead to pay the taxes and buy tax-free municipal bonds and accumulate tax-free interest and invest the money in your personal financial environment. You could just provide a 401(k) plan for your employees without matching funds or safe harbor, and allow your employees to fund their own 401(k) plans or Roth IRAs.

I feel it's important to help my staff understand money and how to become financially free. One of the greatest gifts you can give your employees is to teach them about safe investing so they feel comfortable about being responsible for their own retirement and understand the importance of saving money and getting out of debt.

Rating Your Current Investments

As part of the *Time and Money* game plan, I suggest that you rate your investments on a scale from +10 to -10, with +10 offering the best in maximizing your dollar return, maximizing tax deferral, and effectively utilizing geometric progression. Keep in mind the four basic criteria I presented in Chapter 9, and give investments that meet all four criteria the highest marks. You can regard any material possession that adds meaning to your life as a +10, even though it is not technically an investment. For everything else, the four criteria are:

1. Safety first.
2. Choose assets that show no loss of principal.
3. Choose assets that are always compounding.
4. Choose assets that maximize your tax deferral.

The following chart gives you some specific examples of rating your investments according to these four key criteria.

RATING YOUR INVESTMENTS

+10	Employer-funded retirement accounts; 401(k) with matching dollars; Roth IRAs
+10	Paying off debt; tax-free municipal bonds with after-tax dollars
+9	Qualified pension plans, i.e., 401(k) without matching dollars; traditional IRAs
+10	Owning your home (if it adds meaning to your life)
+10	Owning a second home (if it adds meaning to your life)
+10	Your children's college educations (if this adds meaning to your life)
0	Owning a second home (if it does not add meaning to your life)
-1	Your Porsche car
-3	Your Chevrolet car; a time-share condo
-10	Material possessions that do not add meaning to your life
-10	Consumption that does not add meaning to your life

Some people think it's a good idea to own a wide range of different possessions and investments, but they lack a specific game plan or context to get to economic freedom. Investments or assets bring money into your life, while possessions usually cost you money. Some people believe that certain possessions are investments. Any possession you are still paying for, including your home, is a liability, not an asset. Please note that you get a much higher return on your investment by putting your money into eliminating debt than you would on any other investment of your money except putting matching funds into your 401(k) (remember, only contribute to your 401(k) to the level your employer will match) or your Roth IRA.

The possessions that cost you money receive negative points according to this investment rating system, unless they add meaning to your life. If I bought a Chevrolet, it would be a -3 on my scale. If I bought a Porsche, it would be a -1 because it has a better resale value.

Adding Meaning Versus Being a Good Investment

Many times people experience confusion about how to rate things that add meaning to their lives using this rating system. It is certainly worth owning anything that adds meaning to our lives because we are only here on this planet for a short time. However, this does not mean that anything that adds meaning to our lives would receive a high rating according to this investment rating system.

For example, if your children's college education adds meaning to your life—and certainly to their lives—it receives a rating of +10 even though it is a poor investment in terms of the four basic criteria because the money you spend on your children's education is no longer part of the pool of safe, liquid assets that are invested in safe and geometrically compounding places. The funds you spend on their education will never get a chance to fold over, to use the metaphor for geometric progression from Chapter 6.

According to the rating scale we are using here, a +10 from an investment standpoint is safe and geometrically compounding, it never loses principal, and it maximizes the tax benefit. If you are going to call something an investment, it has to meet this generic description or add meaning to your life on an ongoing basis. There are many things we buy or spend money on that add meaning to our lives in the short term, but we don't call them investments. A vacation to a beautiful tropical island is a case in point.

Some people rationalize purchasing a second home as an investment. What happens is we go skiing in Colorado for a few days and take some time off to look at condominiums. As we walk up to a model unit and knock on the door, a twenty-three-year-old blonde Nordic skier comes out to show us an impeccable condo. And soon he has us thinking he's a tax wizard. He's showing us why we can't afford *not* to buy this place because of all the deductions we will get. Now, at this point, most of us start rationalizing away, because when we want to hear something, reason beats a speedy retreat. The condo is beautiful, and we can easily imagine ourselves coming up here to ski; we see ourselves having lovely times lounging by the fireplace. But almost all of the time, purchasing a vacation home falls somewhere between a 0 and a -5 on the investment scale. It costs you money and takes funds away from your solid, safe, and dependable geometric progression.

Every time you make a large purchase, you lose part of your freedom because you have to spend time and money to store it, insure it, and take care of it. This purchase may be a boat or a vacation home. If you maximize the use of it and it adds meaning to your life, then it is worth the time, effort, and money to have it and merits a high rating. When you stop using it or it no longer adds meaning to your life, then you're better off selling it and putting the money back into liquid assets.

Once, when I lived in Oregon, I did own a beach house, but I owned it free and clear, and I never rented it out. When you own time-shares, you find it's like going to a hotel and discovering that someone has burned a hole in your carpet. It is really discouraging seeing someone else destroy your home. Most of the time, vacation homes or time-shares don't really add meaning to our lives, but we come up with rationalizations to pretend that they do.

Consider whether owning your primary home merits a +10 on the scale because it adds meaning to your life. If you buy a home that doubles in value in five years, it would receive a +4 as an investment unless you find it adds a great deal of meaning. It's nice that your home turned out to be a good investment, but it has nothing to do with your having a strong economic game plan (see Chapter 14 for more about home ownership). We want to keep the things that add meaning to our lives while at the same time developing a powerful economic game plan.

I define anything that is not an investment or does not add meaning to our lives as junk. It can be a house, an old car, gold, silver, or anything else that does not add meaning to our lives. We need to be aggressive about clearing the junk out of our lives. Because we have rationalized so much of our junk, we may deny that it even exists. If something doesn't add meaning to your life, get rid of it! I'll be discussing this more in Part Two, when we look at ways to live in sync with time through greater simplicity.

With every investment, always ask the question: "Does this add meaning to my life?" Again, meaning usually takes precedence over the rate of return because we are only here on this planet for a short time. At a certain point, owning a sailboat may add meaning to your life. When it no longer does, sell the boat and reinvest your money into the investments that are rated +9 or +10.

Remember, your top investments are liquid assets that utilize tax-free or tax-deferred environments such as pension plans, IRAs, and tax-free municipal bonds. One way to reduce your taxes and plan for your retirement is to contribute the maximum amount to your retirement plan—and to your spouse's retirement plan—each year. Even if you have a pension plan or 401(k) at work, both you and your spouse are wise to fund your IRA each year whether it is deductible or not. A Roth IRA would be a +10 on this scale. Use Exercise 7 in Appendix A to rate your current investments.

CHAPTER 12

Investing for Economic Freedom

In the last chapter, we discussed the importance of tax efficiency in your investments, and you rated your investments according to how well they serve you in implementing your game plan for economic freedom. You may be ready to shift some of your existing investments that received lower ratings into areas that meet the four criteria I gave you in Chapter 9. Or you may at long last be following the *Time and Money* game plan of saving and investing your savings in safe, liquid assets that are compounding in a geometric progression.

In this chapter, I will discuss specific strategies for investing for economic freedom as well as describe some of the basic investment opportunities and their advantages and disadvantages. In Chapter 10, I described some of the fundamental risks of the stock market, and by now I'm sure you understand that the *Time and Money* game plan encourages you to avoid risky investments in favor of safe, secure, geometrically compounding investments with a set rate of return.

Basics of Investing

All liquid investments can be classified into two basic categories, equities (stocks) and debt (bonds). In equity investments, the appreciation of capital is based on a positive change in the ratio of buyers to sellers. You need to have more buyers than sellers as well as a perceived demand for the item in question so that the underlying value appreciates. The problem is that you cannot always predict the future ratio of buyers to sellers. Equities include not only stocks but also mutual funds, real estate, rare coins, precious metals, diamonds, collectibles, and commodities. The problem with equities is the lack of predictability. As we look back on recent decades, we see that many people thought that certain equities, such as gold in the 1970s, real estate limited partnerships in the 1980s, and stocks and mutual funds in the 1990s, would never fail and would always go up. This has not been the case.

Debt investments have no appreciation of capital; instead, you become a lender. Debt investments include corporate or municipal bonds, treasury bills, notes, and bonds, government agency bonds, certificates of deposit (CDs), and money market accounts. When you buy bonds, you become the lender; in essence, the borrower is issuing you an IOU. For example, perhaps your county needs to borrow $5 million for city infrastructure improvements and the county government agrees to pay you 4.5 percent until 2013. Even if they decide to refinance that debt and pay it off early, they cannot call in the loan and pay the loan until a particular date in the future. And when this happens, you know exactly what your return will be. The big advantage of debt investments over equities is the predictability of the return on your investment. I only keep debt investments in my portfolio.

Most economic programs deal with probabilities and higher levels of risk than the game plan I've been recommending. Because of this, their results are constantly changing. The *Time and Money* program is a responsible ("response-able") approach. Remember, you will be investing in high-quality liquid assets, and with high-quality liquid assets, you are able to respond appropriately to changing economic conditions. This chapter organizes investment opportunities into two major categories: investment vehicles for pension plans and IRAs, and vehicles for after-tax investments. For both of these, you will want to find a brokerage firm and open a money market account, so we will start with a brief discussion of these important steps.

Selecting a Broker

To buy equities (stocks) or debt investments (bonds), you generally need to work with a broker. To follow the *Time and Money* game plan, which empha-sizes debt investments, you first need to select a brokerage firm that has a large inventory of bonds and that is big enough to be safe and well insured. Most brokers can help you with both treasury bonds and municipal bonds (you'll read more about both of these in the rest of the chapter). Municipal bonds are an inventory item and are bought by brokerage houses and held in their own portfolios in hopes of selling them to you at a higher price than they purchased them for. A large bond inventory increases the likelihood that they will have bonds that fit your selection criteria.

You can purchase bonds at your local bank, at regular brokerage houses, and at bond specialty firms. Large brokerage firms and bond specialty firms usually have the largest inventory, the highest level of expertise, and the greatest degree of safety. Examples of large brokerage firms include A. G. Edwards and Sons, Smith Barney, Merrill Lynch, Paine Webber, Morgan Stanley, Charles Schwab, and Edward Jones. An example of a bond specialty firm would be Griffin, Kubik, Stephens & Thompson out of Chicago, which only sells tax-free municipal bonds.

Next, select a broker who specializes in debt investments such as tax-free municipal bonds, U.S. treasuries, and bank certificate of deposits (CDs) and who will not try to sell you anything else. Don't just take the person who answers the phone at the brokerage house, but instead request someone who is an expert in debt investments.

In selecting a brokerage firm, be sure that it is registered with the National Association of Security Dealers (NASD). You can pretty much assume that the larger firms just mentioned are registered. Find out if the firm is insured and how much insurance there would be on your portfolio. This insurance is provided by the Security Investor Protection Corporation; make sure your portfolio would have at least $500,000 of protection. You can pay to add more insurance. Never go with a brokerage firm that is not insured or registered. Instead, I would suggest going with one of the larger firms mentioned previously.

Once you've narrowed down your selection of brokerage firms, be sure to choose a broker with whom you feel very comfortable, who has expertise in the bond market, and who will follow your instructions and criteria (see Appendix H) in purchasing your bonds. Tell the broker you are only interested in buying AAA-rated tax-free general obligation municipal bonds for your after-tax investments, and only interested in U.S. treasury bonds, government agency bonds, or bank CDs for your tax-deferred pension, 401(k), or IRAs. You are looking for a broker who is knowledgeable and supportive and who follows your instructions. Make sure your broker knows how to update the safety ratings of your bonds and is willing to do so. Every few months, have your broker check your bonds to see if the safety ratings have eroded. Your broker needs to keep you advised on any major changes in the bond world.

When you buy bonds, you may notice that it seems as if no commission is being paid to the broker. Brokers make their money by buying bonds at a discount price from the seller and selling them to you at the market price. Brokers can make from 1 to 3 percent of the amount of the bond. Brokers get very small commissions on municipal bonds, so the biggest problem you will have is making sure your broker doesn't try to talk you into high-commission products. Brokers may also try to sell you municipal bond funds or municipal bond trusts, which have higher commissions and in some cases hidden risks. They can get up to four times the commission plus an annual fee by selling you bond funds. Make sure your broker understands that you do not want bond funds or bond trusts.

Money Market Accounts

To store your money while you are building up enough to purchase your selected bonds, you will want to open a money market account. A money market account works like a bank account where you have a checkbook. You can keep your money in it and write checks against it, although there are often various restrictions. You can always find a money market account to suit you. When you put your money in a money market account, you are buying shares of the money market's investment fund. The share's price does not fluctuate in value the way a share would in stocks or mutual funds. Money market shares are priced at $1 a share. A money market account is similar to a bank savings account, but you get a much higher interest rate.

You can open a money market account at a bank, a full-service brokerage firm, a discount brokerage firm, a mutual fund company, or a credit union. In particular, I would suggest having two money market accounts in the brokerage house you've selected according to the criteria mentioned in the preceding section. You'll use one of these two money markets accounts to store and build up the dividends or interest from your retirement plan until you reinvest it, and the other to build up your after-tax cash assets to a level at which you can purchase tax-free municipal bonds, which we'll be discussing later in the chapter.

Once you have selected a broker, immediately start saving money in your brokerage money market account. I recommend routinely sending a check each month or making an automatic deposit to your brokerage money market account; then, when your account is large enough to purchase a bond, have your broker buy the best bond that meets your criteria. Keep a written log of what you tell your broker and what your broker tells you so you can determine whether he or she is following your instructions. To ensure that the bond the broker describes to you is the same bond that you end up with, verify the details on your receipt. When it comes to your money, it's important that you take full responsibility and become knowledgeable about bonds so that you don't have to rely solely on your broker in the decision-making process.

Investment Vehicles for Pension Plans and IRAs

First, we'll be discussing some of the investment opportunities for your pension plan or IRAs.

United State Treasuries

United States Treasury securities pose little risk when held to maturity because they are backed by the full faith and credit of the United States government. They can be in the form of treasury bonds (eleven-year to thirty-year maturities), notes (two-year to ten-year maturities), or bills (one-month to twelve-month maturities). The cheapest way to buy treasury securities is directly from the government through its treasury direct program (www.trea-surydirect.gov). You can also use a stockbroker, who will charge a small commission, which is negotiable. The longer the maturity dates, the higher the interest you receive. Once you have accumulated enough cash assets, invest where the yield curve flattens, usually at ten-year to fifteen-year maturities (see Chapter 9 for an example of a yield curve). This can vary depending on interest rates. Treasury yields in 2004 are now low, and the yield curve starts flattening at around five to eight years. When ten-year treasury yields are less than 5.5 percent, I pick bonds with a maturity of five to eight years. It's good to invest pension plans and IRAs in treasury notes or bonds, which have advantages over tax-free municipal bonds because you may get up to 1 percent more interest. In addition to United States treasury notes, bonds, and Series EE savings bonds and zero-coupon treasuries, there are Treasury Inflation Protected Securities (TIPS) and Series I savings bonds that provide inflation protection in addition to guaranteed returns.

Government Agency Bonds and Notes

Government agency bonds (United States government-sponsored entities, or GSEs) have an AAA rating because the United States government is considered to have a moral obligation to issue lines of credit if they ever get into trouble. These include bonds from agencies such as the Tennessee Valley Authority, Freddie Mac, and Fannie Mae. These bonds usually pay a higher interest rate than U.S. Treasury bonds.

At this time, I would recommend buying government agency bonds that have a maturity rate of about five to fifteen years. The downside is that you have to pay very close attention to the call feature (the call feature allows the issuer to buy the bonds back before the maturity date if interest rates drop), because many are issued with a one-year call. If you bought them at a high premium and they are called early, you can lose the benefit of the premium paid. Only buy these bonds if they are par (face value) or close to par. Zero coupon government agency bonds are often ideal for Roth IRA contributions because you do not have to worry about what to do with the small annual interest because you only get the interest at maturity.

Bank Certificates of Deposit

Owning a certificate of deposit (CD) is the equivalent of loaning money to a bank; the bank pays you interest, and your money is insured by the United States government against losses of up to $100,000 per bank. I recommend bank certificates of deposit for retirement plans, dividing your investment equally between short-term and long-term options. Focus on investing long-term at ten to fifteen years, wherever the yield curve flattens (recall the diagram in Chapter 9). Never put more than $90,000 in any one bank, in order to give room for the interest to grow. I work with a large brokerage firm, which can pull up on its computers the best interest rates on CDs across the country. This is true with most brokers, but the larger brokers have a greater selection and will probably not go under in times of crisis. The bank pays the broker's commissions on CDs.

Corporate Bonds

If you decide to look into corporate bonds, be sure that you only consider those that are AAA rated. There are very few companies in the United States that have an AAA rating. The problem with corporate bonds is that overnight the rating can change because they are affected by stock market conditions (recall the risks of the market we covered in Chapter 10). History shows us that many bankrupt corporations had good ratings the year before they went under. These bonds are rarely insured, so who is going to pay you when they go bankrupt? Corporate bonds have a default rate five times that of AAA-rated municipal bonds. Another problem is that corporate bonds can be called at any time if there is a reorganization or a merger. For these reasons, I do not recommend corporate bonds. Government agency bonds are better investments than even AAA-rated corporate bonds because of the backing of the U.S. government. In contrast, who are corporations going to draw on if they get into trouble?

Bond Mutual Funds

I would not normally recommend these except for investors who have pension plans where only mutual funds are offered and there are no other options. Bond funds offer a much lower risk than stock funds, but the commissions and fees are higher than with individual bonds. You're better off buying individual bonds.

Vehicles for After-Tax Investments

Now we will look at some of the investment opportunities for your after-tax financial environment.

Tax-Free Municipal Bonds

Municipal bonds are contracts to borrow and lend money; you are the lender and the municipality—for example, the city of Seattle or the state of California—is the borrower. This money is used for projects deemed to be in the public interest. There are a variety of different types of municipal bonds. The one I recommend is a general obligation (G.O.) bond, where the municipality pledges the full taxing power of the municipality to make good on both principal and interest. There are also moral obligation bonds, which do not pledge the taxing power of the municipality. And there are revenue bonds, which are used for projects deemed to be in the public interest but which are not backed by the taxing power of the municipality. Because of the greater level of safety, I recommend only general obligation bonds.

When a municipality issues $200 million in bonds, they are bought by large commercial banks that have underwritten the bond issue. The banks then sell the bonds to brokerage firms in large blocks. The brokerage firms break them down and sell them to clients. These are inventory products, and are also purchased at a discount from individuals who wish to sell their bonds. Brokers make their money from the seller by marking up the price of the bond, and you pay face value for the bond. You do not pay a commission on bonds. You receive a guarantee of collateral to get your money back, and you receive the stated rate of return in a written contract. This is the strongest position you can be in as an investor. Bonds pay interest semiannually (usually in January and July), so with a $10,000 bond paying 5 percent interest, you get $250 twice a year. You can take this compound interest and put it in a money market account and add it to your normal savings until you have another $10,000 to buy another municipal bond. This allows you to compound your investment.

I recommend that you buy bonds in increments of $10,000 or more as opposed to the $5,000 minimum offered by most brokers. Choosing $10,000 denominations increases the number of bonds you can pick from. If you have a large portfolio, you can purchase $25,000 and $50,000 bonds, which will reduce the complexity of your monthly statements.

If you have foreseeable needs for your money in the near future, such as paying taxes or college expenses or making a down payment to buy a house, do not invest in municipal bonds but instead keep your money in your general money market account.

Tax-free municipal bonds are ideal for investors with an income of $50,000 or higher. Because these investors are in a higher tax bracket, they especially benefit from investing their after tax-dollars in a tax-free environment; they also are more likely to have the available money to purchase $10,000 bonds or higher. For those in lower tax brackets who have from $1,000 to $3,000 to invest, long-term CDs, zero coupon government agency bonds, and treasuries provide an alternative.

Be sure to select tax-free municipal bonds with an underlying rating of AA or better. An underlying rating is the true rating of the bond before the bond is insured, which increases its rating. The insurance offers an artificial credit enhancement. I always look at the rating without insurance, because insurance companies are heavily leveraged and engage in other businesses that are much riskier. Around 50 percent of all new bond issues are insured; this is another protection for these bonds and serve as icing on the cake. I don't recommend using tax-free municipal bonds in retirement plans or other tax-deferred environments because you lose their tax advantage. Tell your broker to inform you immediately when your bond is re-rated. This does not happen very often, but if the bond is rated down to A, then you simply sell the bond and get an AAA-rated bond to replace it. The average return over the past fifty years on tax-free municipal bonds has been around 6 percent, resulting in a taxable equivalent yield of 8 to 9 percent (depending on your tax bracket, amount of state income tax, and years to maturity) because you are not paying taxes on the interest earned. The information on taxable equivalent yields in the following charts was taken from a calculator at www.investinginbonds.com. This is an excellent and informative website for learning about debt investments.

REAL YIELDS FOR TAX-FREE MUNICIPAL BONDS

INDIVIDUAL TAX BRACKETS

Interest	15%	25%	33%
1.00%	1.25%	1.45%	1.65%
2.00%	2.50%	2.90%	3.29%
3.00%	3.75%	4.35%	4.94%
4.00%	5.01%	5.80%	6.58%
5.00%	6.26%	7.25%	8.23%
6.00%	7.51%	8.70%	9.87%
7.00%	8.76%	10.14%	11.52%
7.50%	9.39%	10.87%	12.34%

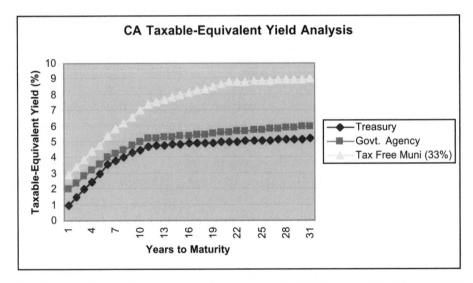

Taxable equivalent yield at various federal tax rates for California residents buying California bonds and assuming both federal and California state income taxes.

When you buy a bond, you know from the very first day the exact terms of the bond. Your confirmation will describe the bond's yield to call (the date when the issuer has the ability to buy back your bond early, prior to the date it matures) as well as the bond's yield to maturity. Currently, interest rates on treasuries are near the lowest in recent history. The interest rates on tax-free municipal bonds are low, but not as low as they have been in the past. In the 1960s, for example, interest rates on tax-free long-term municipal bonds ranged from 3 to 4 percent.

Paying Off Debt or Buying Bonds

Over the past fifty years, the average interest rate on bonds has been around 6 percent. When long-term bond rates of return are lower (less than 5.5 percent), it is better to use your saved after-tax money to pay off debt. When interest yields are between 5.5 and 7 percent, the *Time and Money* plan recommends dividing your savings equally between debt reduction and bonds. But if interest rates go higher (above 7 percent), then put one-third toward debt reduction and two-thirds toward buying ten-year to twenty-year municipal bonds (see the following chart). A great time to purchase twenty-year or thirty-year bonds would have been the early 1980s, when you could get AA-rated noncallable general obligation bonds that were paying 14 percent. When you have bonds paying higher interest, it is important that the bond does not have a call feature (remember, a call feature allows the issuer to buy the bond back earlier if interest rates drop, and you lose the higher interest rate you have enjoyed). Most bonds today have a call feature that protects the issuer and allows the issuer to give you your money back before the maturity of the bond. Issuers do this to cut their losses when interest rates go down after they have issued the bond.

EFFECT OF YIELDS ON BOND MATURITY AND DEBT REDUCTION

Tax-free municipal bond yield rate	Buy bonds with Maturity dates	Percentage of savings put toward debt
Below 5.5%	N/A	Pay down debt
5.5% to 7%	5 to 15 years	1/2 debt – 1/2 bonds
Above 7%	10 to 20 years	1/3 debt – 2/3 bonds

Risks with Municipal Bonds

The primary risk with municipal bonds is that interest rates go up and you might have to sell them before their maturity date. Interest rates are always fluctuating, and when interest rates go up the resale value of your bond goes down to compensate. Interest or resale risk occurs when you have to sell your lower interest bond during a time when bonds are paying a higher interest (yield) rate. If interest rates go up 1 percent, the value of a thirty-year bond drops 12.9 percent, while a ten-year bond's price would fall 6.7 percent and a two-year bond would drop less than 1 percent. For example, suppose you encountered a financial disaster and were forced to sell your 5 percent thirty-year bond in a 7 percent bond market. You could lose from 40 to 50 percent of your principal, depending on the time remaining to the bond's maturity. This is one reason I recommend *against* purchasing bonds with greater than twenty-year maturities. Remember that you will always get your principal by holding your bonds to maturity.

Each year as you invest in bonds that mature where the yield curve flattens, you will automatically be laddering your bonds, meaning that each year you will have bonds maturing. This way you will always have money from these bonds to use for needed expenses or to reinvest in higher yielding bonds if these are available. There is very little chance that AA-rated general obligation bonds or better will ever default. Again, this is a good reason to buy bonds from large reputable brokerage houses.

In cases where you might take a large loss if you had to sell, it would be better to use your brokerage house margin account or borrow the money you need using the bond as collateral. The *Time and Money* game plan does not advise buying municipal bonds until you are well on your way to being out of debt, so this situation will not be likely to arise except in real emergencies. It's always best to hold onto your municipal bonds until maturity. Remember that as bond yields go up, you may see your total portfolio drop, reflecting the value of your bonds if you sold them that day. This is nothing to worry about because you will get the face value of the bonds when you sell them at maturity.

Tax-Free Municipal Bond Selection Criteria

There are certain selection criteria you need to look at when purchasing municipal bonds. These include bond safety, state of origin, whether it's a general obligation bond, and the bond's maturity date and denomination. Appendix H summarizes the basic criteria for investing in tax-free municipal bonds, as well as listing bonds to avoid.

Bond Safety

Bond safety is the most important criterion in purchasing bonds. A high rating does not mean that the bond will not fail, but it does give investors reassurance that the bond is very safe. I recommend AAA-rated general obligation tax-free municipal bonds.

State of Origin

It's generally wisest to buy municipal bonds issued by municipalities within the state where you reside. By doing so, you usually receive a state tax exemption as well as a federal tax exemption on the interest you receive from the bonds. If you reside in a state that has few acceptable bond issuers, has no state income tax, or taxes state bond issues, you may want to consider buying bonds from other states. Check with your broker for your state's specific rules and tax exemptions for municipal bonds.

General Obligation

A general obligation (G.O.) bond is one that pledges the unlimited taxing powers of the municipality to repay a bondholder. General obligation bonds are considered better bonds. Other bonds may give a slightly higher return but come with a disproportionately higher risk.

Bond Maturity Dates and Denominations

The maturity date of a municipal bond tells you how long the municipality will be borrowing your money. If the bond has a ten-year maturity date, you can expect to receive interest for ten years (paid semiannually). At the end of the ten years, you will receive the face value of the bond as payment in full. The face value of the bond is not always the price you paid to buy the bond, depending on the interest rate printed on the bond you have purchased (known as the *coupon rate*) relative to the interest rate being paid in the market at the time you buy the bond. I would recommend focusing on laddering your bonds long-term. When yields are 5.5 percent or less, look at five-year to eight-year maturities, and look at five-year to fifteen-year maturities when yields are above 5.5 percent. As you grow your long-term investments and they eventually start maturing and becoming available for emergencies and reinvesting, you can sell your short-term and low-return investments when they mature and buy more long-term, higher interest bonds.

Ordering Tax-Free Municipal Bonds from a Broker

In this section, I will summarize the procedure for ordering tax-free municipal bonds from your broker. Talk to your broker and show him or her your list of criteria for purchasing municipal bonds (see Appendix H). Once your broker has identified a bond that meets these criteria, you can purchase the bond. After you order the bond, you then have three days to give the brokerage the money; this is called the settlement date, when you start receiving interest.

You will receive a confirmation ticket from the broker to confirm the fact that you own the bond. This ticket shows your account number and your name along with a bond identification number, the date of trade, the settlement date, a description of the bond, the maturity date, any call dates, the bond rating, the dollar price, the principal, and the interest rate. If the confirmation information you receive does not agree with your phone conversation, immediately contact the broker and make sure it is corrected. Each month you will receive a brokerage statement that shows you the name of the bond, the amount of the bond, and any activity that happened with the bond. Be sure to review and reconcile each of these statements.

The chart in Appendix H summarizes the basic principles for you to review so you can be sure your broker follows them when recommending bonds to you.

CHAPTER 13

Increasing Income and Enjoying Life Now

Most people who start new businesses or new careers don't have a context to save money or a game plan for economic freedom. No matter how much they make over the years, they unconsciously find a way to spend it all. They have somehow developed the belief that they will never be able to save enough money, even though their income since they first entered the work world has gone up four to five times. Some people believe they cannot become economically free in their own business or through their own income from work. I have seen people do all kinds of things to try to make it on the side. Their rationale is, in essence, "I can't make it in what I am doing, so I will do something I don't know how to do and make it." I heard of an orthopedic surgeon who bought the rights to a donut franchise for the whole state of Alaska. He started his first franchise near an army base. He managed to lose $1.5 million before he went broke. Some people who thought they were masters in the stock market lost up to 90 percent of their retirement portfolio in the recent crash and now have to start all over.

Making Your Money through Work

We can always make enough money in our own business or in our own line of work if we have the right context. First, we need to figure out what we do well, then set what we do well up in a context where it is profitable, and then do more of it. Take a percentage of what you make and store it in a geometrically progressing retirement plan or personal financial environment, use the rest to live on, and you will reach economic freedom. Remember, it takes very little to get a large result. Typically, reaching economic freedom does not require making more money but rather organizing our money and debt to create a context where our cash flow is operating efficiently.

Some people who have been working a long time start feeling depressed because they don't have a solid game plan for reaching economic freedom. Instead of reorganizing their work lives to make them exciting, efficient, and profitable, they do other things to create excitement. They prefer taking a tremendous risk to get 20 or 30 percent on their investments, and they usually end up losing their money.

Many people feel they will make more money investing than they do out of earnings. This is 100 percent wrong. If you had $100,000 invested properly, you would be making about 5 percent a year, or $5,000. Your ability to earn money is more valuable than any amount of money you have. Our main source of money is earning it and then storing it. We are not going to get rich on investments, but it's important to invest wisely. The greatest power we have is our earning power. After ten or fifteen years, the money we put away will become very large, even if we have it invested conservatively. The reality is that at any time we can change our mindset and make our work fun and exciting. We can even hire good coaches to help us make our work lives more efficient and profitable.

Today we live much longer than our parents, and we have many different opportunities and career choices. If we can set up our work lives to be fun and enjoyable, most of us will continue to work part-time well into our so-called retirement years. This reduces our anxiety and the need for such a large retirement nest egg. If we change our mindset about retirement and realize that it, too, is a process, we'll see we have greater opportunities to live full lives now and in our senior years.

Increasing Your Income as an Employee

Here are some ideas for increasing your income. The best investment is to spend money for your personal and professional growth. If you invest $50,000 to go to school and this allows you to increase your income by $50,000, this would be worth $1 million over twenty years. You can make yourself so valuable that you can ask for a raise or charge your customers more. Any time you get a raise or bonus, automatically save it.

Significantly Increasing Your Net Profit as a Business Owner

Over my years as a financial advisor, I have worked with many professionals, mostly doctors. Like all other businessmen and businesswomen, doctors face similar issues of business management, preparing for retirement, and economic freedom.

In my coaching, I have found that many physicians, dentists, and other business owners are more interested in engaging in their profession than in taking time to set up an efficient business model. I highly recommend that such professionals hire a coach who is familiar with their business and who has a good track record of success. I have found that just by modifying a few things in a practice, professionals can often double their net profit. Having systems in place to schedule patients more efficiently, collecting fees at the time of service, emphasizing more profitable procedures, and raising fees are all examples that significantly increase the bottom line without raising overhead.

As an example, if a doctor's overhead is 70 percent and she increases her fees by only 15 percent, this will result in a 50 percent increase in her paycheck. How would you like an additional 50 percent of your income available for debt reduction, for savings, and for investing in your Roth IRA and tax-free municipal bonds? See the following chart to get a sense of what a difference increasing your fees can make. You can also trade the fee increase for time. In this scenario, you could work one-third less time and produce the same income.

HOW INCREASED FEES AFFECT NET INCOME

OVERHEAD	PERCENTAGE OF FEE INCREASE			
	5%	10%	15%	20%
	Increase in net income			
80%	25.0%	50.0%	75.0%	100.0%
75%	20.0%	40.0%	60.0%	80.0%
70%	16.6%	33.0%	50.0%	66.6%
65%	14.3%	28.6%	42.9%	57.2%
60%	12.5%	25.0%	37.5%	50.0%
55%	11.1%	22.2%	33.3%	44.4%
50%	10.0%	20.0%	30.0%	40.0%

Enjoying Life Now

When we get to be between forty and fifty years old, our lives change. Many of us go through a clinical depression because we have lost the excitement of starting our careers or our practices. Things may be going smoothly. The kids may be in college. But we may find that life changes even if we don't want to admit it. We don't make changes in our work life anymore, and we don't care if it gets any better; we just hope it doesn't get any worse. Sometimes we take up hobbies instead of creating excitement in our work lives. As we reach midlife, it's time to realize that this is it, that it's not going to get any better, that it's all in our minds. We need to realize this is an opportunity to go to work happy every day and to change our relationship to work so that it is fun. Life can be exciting if we let it.

The future does not exist except in our imaginations, and the past is merely a tracing in our minds. The brain changes our recollections to fit our own convenience and purposes. This is also true with our work lives. Once we understand that we are working on a day-to-day basis, not a year-to-year basis, our attitudes and philosophies change, and incidentally we become more prosperous and have more fun.

I have consistently found that those who were happy while they were working are also happy during their retirement years. The opposite is also true: those who did not enjoy their work don't find happiness in retirement any more than they did while they were working.

I once had a fifty-year-old client from North Carolina. He told me that he had hated dentistry for the past twenty-five years. The worst problem was that he could not quit because he owed so much money. I told him that I could set up his finances so he would be economically free in ten years.

I knew his problem was deeper than finances, so I asked him, "Once you reach economic freedom, what are you going to do?"

"I would first quit my practice," he told me.

"Then what are you going to do?" I asked.

"I am going to golf," he replied.

"Then what are you going to do?"

He said, "I will buy a place on the beach and walk on the beach."

"Great," I said. "Then what are you going to do?"

"Then I will watch TV and read books."

"Then what are you going to do?" I asked him one more time.

He became really sad and somber and said, "I will just walk on the beach some more."

"Great! What are you going to do then?"

He started to cry and said, "I'm going to die."

This is a pretty sad story. There was no real aliveness to this man, just a dead story. What my fifty-year-old client was trying to do was to get someplace instead of loving his life. I told him, "My job is to assist you in knowing that life is never going to be any better or worse than it is right now. It's just how you're looking at it. For you to go back and spend one more day losing your life for some future time which does not sound all that exciting will make your life a failure." He did not like hearing this, but he knew it was true. So I told him to go home, and I asked him to promise me that he would change his mind and outlook so he could enjoy dentistry again and appreciate his patients, his staff, and all his relationships. If he did this and found he still did not enjoy dentistry, then he would quit and sell everything and do something in life that he enjoyed.

My dentist friend did go back, and he began to enjoy his practice. I coached him to slow down and sell some things to get rid of his debt, and he finally started to relax. Because life is in the present, it will truly never get any better or worse than it is this minute. It's all a matter of how we look at our experiences with life. This principle is the same for each and every one of us.

Another client, Jim, was an orthopedic surgeon and looked very young even at age sixty-five. Jim was generally a very happy man, but when he came into my office one day he looked terrible and told me that he was in real trouble. He said that because of his employment contract, he had to retire next year. I told him I thought that was great. He said his group had set up a pension plan just six years ago, and he had only $300,000 in it. Jim's eyes started to water, and he reached into his pocket and pulled out a legal sheet that was folded and soiled and worked over. "I've been working for two weeks and I haven't slept much. My game plan for retirement is to live the next four years better than the last four, and then I will be broke."

I told him there might be a more satisfying way to approach this and asked him to make an appointment in two weeks so we could develop a better plan for him. When he came for his next appointment, we developed a game plan of first using his personal financial environment to live on, including a reverse mortgage on his home. He was also able to work part-time one day a week. By doing this, he kept his pension plan in geometric progression so it could grow to a point of economic freedom very easily. Jim's case was particularly interesting. During our annual meeting twelve years later, he was economically free and enjoying the process of living life day by day.

CHAPTER 14

Owning a Home and Paying Off the Mortgage Early

In our younger years, it is probably better to rent a home rather than to buy one. For the same amount of money you would spend on a mortgage, you can usually rent a much larger house or apartment. In addition, you do not have to worry about paying taxes or repair bills. You can set this additional money aside so you can make a larger down payment on a home when you're ready to buy one. With a larger down payment, your monthly mortgage payment will be much lower.

The younger generation today is much more mobile than earlier generations, and there is a good chance you will change jobs and move to a different location, perhaps more than once. Renting gives you much more flexibility, and you can move at any time without the worry or expense of selling a house. Ownership reduces your options, since selling the house after only two or three years can result in a net loss. Because housing markets routinely go up and down, by renting you'll be able to wait until housing prices are down to buy. With the money you have saved for your down payment while renting, you'll be able to get the house you desire at a great price.

When you reach the point in your life where you're ready to settle down in one place for a longer period, it becomes worthwhile to consider buying a house. Throughout the years, my home has added meaning to my life. As I've indicated earlier, it's not a good idea to acquire real estate unless it adds meaning to your life. Eventually, most people do find owning their home very meaningful.

Your Home as an Investment

Your home is almost always your largest single purchase, and the cost can be two to three times greater than it needs to be because of mortgage interest. Most homeowners don't consider accelerating their mortgage payments because no one else they know is doing it. In this chapter, I'll lay out the tremendous advantages of paying off your mortgage early.

At the most basic level, a home is not really an investment, though home ownership does add meaning to our lives and protects us against inflation because the price of a house almost always goes up with inflation. In the 1950s, 1960s, and 1970s, there was a large appreciation in home values. This isn't necessarily the case these days, although in a few geographical areas prices continue to rise substantially. In general, however, there are not as many buyers to purchase homes as there once were, which has slowed the increase in prices. Also, the tax breaks we get on owning a home are not what they used to be before the tax reform of 1986. The small tax breaks we get on mortgage interest only slightly reduce the effect of interest costs.

Real estate agents and accountants often advise you to buy the biggest house that you possibly can to save money on your taxes, even if you can barely afford it. This is bad advice for many reasons. There are many more effective ways to reduce your taxes, especially through investing in Roth IRAs and pension plans. If your income goes down for any reason and you have tied yourself into a huge mortgage, you might find yourself under great stress to meet your monthly payment. During stressful economic times, many people lose their homes. This need never happen if you follow the *Time and Money* game plan. Buying a bigger house than you really need leaves you with fewer resources for getting out of debt and investing in your game plan for economic freedom. Because money issues destroy many relationships, why overstretch? It is much better to buy a comfortable house that you can easily afford, freeing up additional money to put into your savings and investments. Then paying off your mortgage early will allow you to focus on enjoying your relationship while you make rapid progress toward economic freedom.

Paying Off Your Mortgage Early

According to the National Association of Realtors, the average family changes homes every seven years. The problem is that after seven years with a typical thirty-year mortgage, homeowners have paid off only about 8 percent of the balance. This means they still owe 92 percent on their home. If they trade their home up for another 100 percent mortgage every seven years, this would mean that after twenty-one years they would still owe 92 percent on their mortgage. On the other hand, if they paid off the mortgage in seven years, they would own their home free and clear and be able to put hundreds of thousands of dollars into investments.

Most people think they have a 7 percent mortgage, but this is only true if they pay the mortgage off in the first twelve months. In the example I just gave, most people with a thirty-year mortgage are paying 87 percent of the payment toward interest the first year, which slowly goes down to 76 percent toward interest the tenth year. This means they do not have a 7 percent loan but an 87 percent loan that goes down to a 76 percent loan by the tenth year.

In general, it's a good idea to pay off your mortgage as soon as possible. I recommend having a thirty-year mortgage but increasing the monthly payments so that you pay off your house in five to nine years. If the price of your home is within your means, you can easily do this once you've paid off all the rest of your consumer debt.

When you are deciding on the size of your house, I recommend that you buy a home that you can easily afford to pay off within a fifteen-year mortgage. Your house payment including principal, interest, and insurance should add up to no more than 28 percent of your monthly *take home* pay. If you earn over $150,000 a year, your house payment should be no more than 16 percent of your monthly *take home* pay (this may not be realistic in some geographical areas). As you start paying down debt according to the *Time and Money* game plan, you will free up additional "found money" from your paid-off debts and can use this to pay your mortgage off early.

Just as an example, paying off your $250,000 home with a 7 percent interest rate in fifteen years instead of thirty years saves you $194,299. Paying it off in seven years saves you $281,826.

$250,000 HOME WITH 7% INTEREST RATE				
Years of mortgage	Monthly payments	Additional monthly payment	Interest paid	Interest saved
30-year	$1,663	$0.00	$348,772	$0.00
15-year	$2,247	$584.00	154,473	$194,299
7-year	$3,773	$2,110.00	$66,946	$281,826

As I mentioned earlier, some advisors suggest that you buy a bigger house and pay more interest because you can write it off on your taxes. This is just as smart as going to the bank and asking them to give you a higher interest loan. In reality, if you are in a 25 percent tax bracket, you can only write off 25 percent of the interest, so you are still paying 75 percent extra interest. Is it worth paying $75 to save $25 in taxes? In the example of the $250,000 home I just gave, if you pay off your home in seven years, you would have a savings of $281,826. After you've paid off your house, you will have an additional $3,773 to invest conservatively at 8 percent in a retirement plan that will yield $2,237,623 in twenty years or $5,539,209 in thirty years.

To help you see how much money you could save by paying off your mortgage early, go to the Kansas City Life Calculator found online at www.mortgagecalc.com or at http://www.kclife.com/calculations.aspx. The following charts give you an idea of how much you can save by paying off your mortgage early. If you increase your mortgage payment by 50 percent on a fifteen-year mortgage and by 100 percent on a thirty-year mortgage, you can have your home paid for in five to nine years (see the following charts). When you pay off any loan, the amount of interest you are paying is equal to receiving the same amount of money tax-free. If you pay off a 7 percent loan, it's as if you are getting the equivalent of a 9 to 10 percent return on your money.

				Paid off		Total
Interest	Money saved	Monthly payment	Extra monthly payment	in # of years	15 years of interest	15-year cost
6%	$60,738	$2,110	$1,050	8.4 years	$129,736	$379,736
7%	$76,892	$2,247	$1,150	8 years	$154,473	$404,473
8%	$92,819	$2,389	$1,200	7.8 years	$180,043	$430,043
9%	$111,940	$2,536	$1,300	7.5 years	$206,420	$456,420

LOAN AMOUNT $250,000   15-YEAR MORTGAGE

Increasing monthly principal payments by 50 percent pays off the loan in 7.5 to 8.4 years.

LOAN AMOUNT $250,000   30-YEAR MORTGAGE

				Paid off		Total
Interest	Money saved	Monthly payment	Extra monthly payment	in # of years	30 years of interest	30-year cost
6%	$215,350	$1,499	$1,500	9 years	$289,595	$539,595
7%	$270,062	$1,663	$1,700	8.1 years	$348,772	$598,772
8%	$324,785	$1,834	$1,800	7.8 years	$410,388	$660,388
9%	$385,936	$2,012	$2,000	7 years	$474,160	$724,160

Increasing monthly principal payments by 100 percent pays off the loan in 7 to 9 years.

I recommend that you build up your liquid assets and pay off small debt *before* you start making extra payments on your house. Then, if the country goes into an economic depression, you can still make your payments on your house using your saved liquid assets. With a thirty-year mortgage, your payments are low enough that you can ride out hard times. Following the *Time and Money* game plan, once you have paid off any credit card debt and funded your IRA and retirement accounts, you can start paying down your mortgage by sending in additional money each month toward the loan principal. Having your home paid off is one of the richest feelings there is. I highly recommend paying off your mortgage before you retire. It's even better to own your house while you're young!

CHAPTER 15

Insurance, Estate Planning, and Avoiding Financial Mistakes

Once you put the *Time and Money* philosophy into practice by saving 20 percent of your income and investing reliably in safe, liquid, geometrically progressing assets, you will inevitably reach economic freedom. As long as you're working, I can assure you that you will get this result because you have your earning power to rely upon.

Insurance

As I mentioned earlier, only two things can prevent your game plan for economic freedom from working: if you become disabled and are no longer able to work, or if you die. These are the circumstances for which you need insurance. Please note that life insurance and disability insurance are not investments. You buy them only to replace money that you and your family would need if you became disabled or died. Once you have enough liquid assets to provide your income for the rest of your life—that is, once you have reached economic freedom—you can safely cancel your life insurance and disability insurance policies and instead put the money that would have gone toward your insurance premiums into safe, liquid, compounding assets.

Life Insurance

Life insurance is an important part of your financial plan. Most insurance companies will insure you up to ten to fourteen times your income depending on how old you are. To protect your family, I recommend that you buy as much life insurance as you qualify for for as long as you need it. Once you are economically free, buying insurance is inappropriate consumption. Only buy cheap term insurance. It is important to select a reputable life insurance company that has good returns and a high Weiss safety rating. One of the strongest life insurance companies is Northwestern Mutual. If you have a life insurance policy now, continue to maintain it. If you need more coverage, supplement it with term or blended insurance. Once you reach the point where you are financially free and owe no debt, you can drop your term insurance. Before canceling any insurance policy, be sure to get a good physical examination. If you know you are likely to die soon, keep your life insurance because then it is a good deal.

Disability Insurance

Many financial advisors encourage professionals to obtain disability insurance. The problem is that there are very few companies that provide good disability insurance. You would want to find a disability insurance that is guaranteed renewable and cannot be canceled. To reduce the premiums, you might want to extend the limitation out ninety or 180 days. Again, once you become financially free, my recommendation is that you dispense with disability insurance.

Health Insurance

Another troubling area is health insurance. Premiums have skyrocketed over the past few years, and good insurance costs a great deal. Hopefully your workplace offers good health insurance coverage. If you're out on your own, one way to reduce your premiums is to purchase only catastrophic insurance coverage that has a $5,000 or a $10,000 deductible and to invest the money you save on premiums in your personal health coverage savings account to cover you up to the deductible. It costs the average American $500,000 to die without health insurance, which can eat up a big portion of your estate, so it's worth having this safety net.

Other Insurance

You get better rates on homeowner's insurance if you choose a higher deductible. Make sure that you are not overinsured or underinsured for your geographical area. I recommend a $1 million or $2 million-dollar umbrella insurance policy (often available as a rider to a homeowner's insurance policy) to protect you and your family against personal lawsuits. It is very inexpensive and provides peace of mind.

Of course, there are also legally mandated types of insurance, including auto insurance and liability insurance for certain professions. Again, remember that these are not investments, but they provide protection for your assets as well as peace of mind; you will generally get better rates if you choose higher deductibles.

Estate Planning

Estate planning is an important part of the *Time and Money* financial game plan because it helps you reach economic peace of mind. As an overview, everyone needs at least a simple will. As you gain more assets, get married, or seek to protect your property from unnecessary taxes, you need a more comprehensive will. Find a good estate attorney to draw up this will and be sure to include a revocable living trust. Remember that the beneficiaries of your IRA retirement accounts, annuities, life insurance policies, and trusts are named directly by you and are not part of the will. If you get divorced and remarry, or other significant circumstances change, it may be important to change your beneficiaries for all these areas.

In addition to a will and a revocable living trust, it's important to have your attorney draw up a general power of attorney authorizing someone to handle your financial affairs if you are unable to do so. The person you name needs to be someone you trust completely; this is usually your spouse or another relative. In case you become sick and are unable to make decisions, you are wise to have a living will along with a durable power of attorney for health care set up in advance. This gives someone you name the legal rights to make medical decisions for you. Most people choose a spouse or another trusted family member.

Take time to sit down with your family and talk about your estate plan long before you become ill. Let your family have some input about who gets what, and let them know your wishes for what happens after you die. I highly recommend that you complete a form letting your family know where your important papers are, what assets you have, and who your important advisors are. Be specific about what you want done with your remains. Exercise 8 in Appendix A and the chart in Appendix F will help you organize this information.

Avoiding Financial Mistakes

In this section, I will outline some of the basic financial mistakes you'll want to be sure to avoid.

Never Make Big Financial Mistakes

The most important way to keep your wealth is never to make a big financial mistake. Big financial mistakes usually occur because of greed and ego. I have seen some of my clients lose their entire portfolios in get-rich-quick schemes. Such schemes range from real estate deals to limited partnerships or just about anything else that sounds too good to be true. Remember, there is no free lunch. When you have a systematic game plan to put your money into safe liquid assets that will make you economically free in a fairly short time, why would you want to take a risk on anything else? If you just stick with the boring *Time and Money* philosophy of investing, you'll never put your retirement money at risk.

Do Not Fail to Stop and Find Out What Makes You Happy

The things that really make me happy and that I enjoy doing are very simple and cost almost nothing. If I had known this earlier at the deepest level, I would not have had to drive myself so hard to be successful. This is why the process of writing a new story (see Exercise 5 in Appendix A) is so important. Write down what you would like your average day to look like. What are the things that make you happy? Don't include shopping! What are the happiest times you've enjoyed in your life? When you know who you are, it is easy to save money. Usually the simplest and least expensive things make you happy. Try to spend the least amount of money trying to figure out what makes you happy. Rent your way through the discovery process (for example, rent that lovely condo in the mountains rather than buy it). Most people live a life of high debt and stress because they spend money hoping it will make them happy. I guarantee you that it is not money or things that will give you peace or happiness.

Never Lease Equipment or Automobiles

Never lease equipment in your business. Leasing is very costly, and the interest can be up 31 percent. If you miss a single payment, some leasing companies can completely repossess the equipment, and you are still liable for the monthly payments. At the end of most leases, you have to buy the equipment back for an additional 10 percent or ship it back to the company at your expense.

The conditions for leasing an automobile are not as bad as leases on equipment, but I still would not lease a car. You will spend between $2,500 and $4,000 more to lease a $30,000 car than if you were just to borrow the money and pay for it. Average lessees pay 8 percent more on the sticker price of an automobile, and this does not include the interest. They would be better off borrowing the money, paying cash, and negotiating about the price. On the spectrum of evils, one of the worst things you can do is lease anything. If you do buy a car, I recommend buying one that is one to two years old, which allows you to save 20 to 30 percent of the initial price.

The worst thing you can lease is technology. Renting and leasing are significantly different. Renting involves making payments each month; you can stop at any time. Leases feel as if they are for life. It is painful, expensive, and time-consuming to get out of a lease, and the effective annual interest rate in leases is often exorbitant.

Beware of Lending Money

If you lend money to friends or family, please realize there is a good possibility you will never be repaid. Often this will have a negative impact on the relationship. If lending the money is meaningful to you, then consider just giving it as a gift.

CHAPTER 16

Giving and Serving

Some people have a difficult time giving. Perhaps they are afraid of ending up with nothing, but the truth is, the more you give, the more you get. Givers win, and takers lose. Giving goes back a long way. The philosopher Aristotle once said that if you want to understand something, go back to its beginnings. As early human beings went out into the savannas, one of the most important things for tribal survival was learning to give. Giving is instinctively imprinted in our DNA. Because the plains were a dangerous place, early humans learned to share their food. This was one of the symbols of belonging in the tribe and helped bond each person to the group. Giving was necessary for survival because when you were unsuccessful in your hunt, someone else would give you and your children food so that you would not starve. The mutual benefits of giving are part of our human legacy.

The Joy of Giving

Modern human beings have created a new standard by which the one with the most sheep, money, or "toys," as some put it, wins. Operating under this context, people think, "If I give, I won't have as much, and I'll lose power." So they start storing the excess instead of giving it to others. But the truth is that you can still win and give. I have always given instinctively. When I started my practice, I hired a woman named Rhoda as my secretary. She knew that I was successful in what I did, but it terrified her that I was always giving money away and raising salaries. I see myself as a conduit for bringing money in and sharing it, and I just love it. This is part of my joy in life. Over a period of time, Rhoda came to see that all of this giving creates a wonderful spirit. She could also see that I always had abundance.

When I met my partner, Lori, we would sometimes walk into the slums of Portland and panhandlers would come up to me and ask for money. I would ask them how much they wanted, and I just loved giving money to them. But Lori was from a family that did not give money to panhandlers and instead acted as if they were lepers. She was shocked that I would do this. What most people don't understand is that when panhandlers ask for money, they are simply doing their job. This is how they make their living. It is ridiculous to take this as some kind of insult.

I remember once when Lori and I were in Portland early in our relationship, and a shadowy figure emerged from a building. I invited him over. He was a very short Native American wearing a stocking cap and eating a potato, and he was a bit drunk. He looked up at me, which was really unusual, and said, "Can I have some money?"

"Sure," I replied. "How much do you want?"

He thought about this for a moment and replied, "Two dollars."

I pulled out my wallet and gave him two dollars. He stuck the money in his pocket, stood there for a few moments, and then his eyes started to fill with tears. He came up and put his arm under my arm and began to tell me about his parents and his tribe. He told me he was an Indian and felt funny about asking for money. I told him how wonderful it was that he was so successful in his job. He got through the story and talked with me for about ten minutes, and then looked up at me and said, "By the way, do you have any money?"

I said, "Sure, would you like some?" I gave him two more dollars, and he told me another story. This happened about six times, because he kept forgetting that he had already asked me for money.

Another time we were walking around the same area and a big Indian came up to me and asked me for money. I asked him how much and gave him what he asked for. Then two of his friends came out of the side alley and joined us. What was interesting was that they got so much into the experience of talking about their heritage that they forgot to ask for money. These have always been phenomenal experiences for me.

Giving Is for You

As I mentioned, I see myself as a conduit in my giving. Giving is not for somebody else. It is for you. Money is a good thing to start with; try to give money away as much as you can to get in the habit of giving. If you do this, you will absolutely never go dry. Once we learn to give money, we can start learning to give love. The same principle applies with love: the more you love, the more love you get back. Everything you give, you get back in bountiful supply.

Serving

One of the great turning points in my life was to become unconditionally committed to serving people. I've grown incredibly as a result of this. All of us have the incredible opportunity every day to serve people completely and without conditions. When we serve and let go of our egos, we create the opportunity to grow and come clean.

When you are totally clean, you know because people are willing to serve you. The only thing that stands in the way of great service is usually yourself. When you're interacting with someone who is impatient, you can become patient and that is serving. Serving is not buying into or reacting to other people's problems, but rather showing a total commitment to taking care of them and loving them.

We can see the extent of our brain damage, or childhood and cultural programming, by observing how we serve people. When we are totally and unconditionally committed to service, we give with no expectation of getting anything back. Then our state of mind is absolutely clean.

If you want to see what you still have to work on in your mind, observe your service. If you resent serving, it is not about those you are serving; it's about you. If you are shy, embarrassed, or never go the whole way in your service, this simply tells you where you still have healing to do. All of the people you meet have a totally different computer filled with programming on their shoulders, so each one gives you a new and unique opportunity to serve yourself through growth. The opportunity to grow is absolutely incredible in this arena.

Giving freely and serving unconditionally will only add to your context of economic freedom, abundance, and prosperity.

CHAPTER 17

Money and Children

Our children learn from observing us and not from what we tell them. Our own behaviors around economics send the most powerful messages. Wise parents set time aside to help their children create a clear context about money and to develop a prosperity mindset.

As your children get older, encourage them to get a part-time job and set up a bank account. Then show them the power of geometric progression in a tax-deferred environment such as a Roth IRA. Instill in them the importance of saving part of everything they make, possibly 25 percent. When your children see that money is as natural as air and water, they learn that it can flow effortlessly into their lives. When they're in high school, they can see the money growing in their bank accounts. This positive reinforcement feels really good. If you follow these simple steps, your children will always feel appropriately nurtured and at peace with money. The money your children have invested in their accounts is not for spending on college, because you've been growing their college fund in a separate account.

Funding Your Children's Education

The best way to save for your children's college education is to invest in high-grade tax-free municipal bonds in your name in your personal after-tax investment environment. By the time your children are ready to go to college, you can fund their education just by using the tax-free interest from the bonds, allowing you access, control, and ownership of the money. Remember, the principal is your retirement money and you will need it later. Most of us worked and took out loans for our college educations and felt a good sense of responsibility by doing so. Our children can do the same, so it's up to you what percentage of your children's education costs you wish to fund.

Be cautious with regard to recently instituted government-run 529 plans. These are municipal- and state-issued plans to fund college educations. These plans sound incredible, but come with some major problems. The tax benefits sound wonderful, but they are not smart investments because you are trapped into a very few investment choices. You have very little choice in the investment strategy of the state; if the investment drops in value, you lose that money. Also, there is no guarantee that benefits will last beyond 2010, when the recent changes in tax law expire.

Avoiding Manipulation

Another gift you can give to your children is not to manipulate them and not to let them manipulate you about money. Manipulation involves a controller and someone being controlled, and the person being controlled almost always resents it. All of us appreciate clean, fair guidelines, and children are no different. If you have enough money, you can be very generous with your children. Set up a context that works for you, and only give your children the amount of money that feels good to you.

If you are constantly bailing your children out, you make money slippery for them and then they learn that money is slippery. Once you have helped them set up a solid game plan around money, if they run out of money and no one comes to the rescue, they will figure out an answer by responding naturally. This will help give them a sense of control over money and over their lives.

I would recommend that you and your children decide how much they will need or what you can afford for their college educations and that you put this money in their accounts yearly over four years. Tell them this is the last money they will receive from you but that there will be no stipulation on how they spend it. You will only offer advice on managing it if they ask you, and they can spend it any way they want, including on their educations, without any judgment on your part. However, make it very clear that this money is all they are going to get.

Teaching your children to have integrity with money is one of the most powerful gifts you can give them.

Dealing with Different Parenting Styles

In the same family, one parent may have a prosperity mindset and feel open to giving the children money without caring whether the children work or not. The other parent may feel that it's important to teach children how to work hard so the parents won't end up having to take care of their children for the rest of their lives. If you're the one who feels the children need to work, you may feel unsupported, angry, and resentful at your spouse for making you look like the bad guy. If there are differences in your parenting styles around money, it's best to be open with your children and tell them that it's okay that each of you has a different approach to handling money or work. As your children move into adulthood, they will realize that everyone has different attitudes and feelings about money.

Differences among Your Children

It seems in every family there is almost always one child who needs more money than the others. Giving disproportionate amounts of money to our children can cause bad feelings. All children want to be treated equally, and they see it as a fairness issue. It's not just about money but about love. I suggest having regular family meetings to show your children openly what each of them is going to receive and where each of them stands. Remind them that it will all even out over time.

Remember, from a historical perspective, a couple of hundred years ago rich aristocrats considered it embarrassing for their children to work. It was a matter of status that they distribute their money so their children would not have to work. Our modern culture has switched this around so that we think that people who don't work are bums. In fact, not having to work is great, and having to work is great, too. It is important to clear up these issues because it's unhealthy to have secrets in your family.

Dealing with Inheritance

Some people feel that giving their children too much will spoil them and rob them of the skills they need to develop to sustain themselves. This is an illusion. By the time children are seven years old, they are already programmed to do what they're going to do. I believe that children who are growing up in a family that has abundance deserve to be part of the abundance. After my dad started making money, he was very selfish with it. Everything he did was for himself, and he did not share his abundance with me. This was just another issue I needed to work through and let go of when it came to developing integrity with money, but at the time it felt like another abandonment. I have handled money very differently with my own children.

Over the past forty years, I have had many chances to see how people try to control their children with inheritance money. Money is power, and money is control. When I was practicing law, I had a client come in and tell me, "When my daughter is forty, she should be reasonably competent, and then she can have the money." In such a case, what may very well happen is that the client's daughter will become a bum because she knows she will be rich when she is forty. She won't have had the opportunity to learn any skills for dealing with money. She'll reach the age of forty without knowing how to handle money, which will increase the chances that she'll blow it and live in poverty. Give your children the money now! If they're going to blow the money, let them get it over with so they can still do something useful with their lives.

The bottom line is that it's important for us to teach our children to have integrity with money instead of just giving them money. The inheritance I give my children flows from the philosophy of respect and integrity with money that I've been sharing with them all along. They don't even have to pay taxes on it. It's good to give children the opportunity to manage money and look out for their own interests. In working with the older children of my clients, I've found that all too often money issues are interfering with their relationships. I advise parents to address these money issues early. Just tell them, "Here is your money, and do not plan on getting another cent from me." Then the relationship becomes real instead of being based on money. In Part Two, we'll explore the principles of coming into sync with time and of living with simplicity, both of which can also enrich your relationship with your children and become part of the inheritance you pass on to them.

PART TWO

Time:
Living with Simplicity

CHAPTER 18

About Time

Time is a human concept; it has no absolute reality. We human beings have created various demarcations of time—years, months, weeks, days, hours, and minutes—for our own convenience. These demarcations have varied from culture to culture; they are not absolutes, although they are usually based on the planet's rotation around the sun and the cycles of the moon. Some people say they do not have enough time, but you can only have the amount of time that exists! You cannot make time and you cannot save it, because time is an illusion. If you could save time, where would you put it?

Perspectives on Time

Our cultural ideal is to live in a little white cottage and rest; all too often, when we actually reach that point, we start living on automatic.

The more automatic our days are, the faster our lives go by. The reason so many old people think that time is speeding up and their lives are slipping away is that they are on automatic most of the time. When we have new experiences, our perspective on time shifts, which actually lengthens our lives. You can live the equivalent of ten years longer than most people by embracing an appropriate perspective on time. When you go off automatic and really pay attention to the details, your life becomes longer because time is only a matter of perspective. An easy way to imagine this is to remember what it's like when you're traveling and you take a wrong turn. You go farther and farther, and then you realize you're on the wrong road and you've been on it for a long time. But when you turn around and go back to where you took the wrong turn, your trip seems much shorter. This is because the terrain is already somewhat familiar, so you're already a bit on automatic.

We cannot save time, but we can rearrange it. Typically, we try to fit time to our lives, which does not work at all. We need to learn to fit our lives to time! If you're going to live in the present and enjoy each moment to the fullest, you have to fit your life to the code of time. All too often, we fall into the habit of trying to force too many activities into a given time frame. When we don't get everything done, we become anxious. If we repeat this pattern often enough, we find we are living in a state of near-constant anxiety. So instead of trying to increase the amount of time we have—which isn't possible anyway—we're better off adjusting ourselves with integrity to the time we've been given.

The Key: Simplify Your Life

The only way you can live your life fully and with integrity regarding time is to get in sync with time moment by moment. Whether I'm working or playing, I don't put too many activities into my life. I've learned I can choose the activities I want in my life, and so can you. All of our lives are eventually going to come to an end. We need to stop making excuses for not enjoying the time we have and begin to live life fully right now, because this is it!

Most people cram way too much into their days. Part of this is cultural. Cultural ideals tell us that we should exercise more, that we should work outside the home even if we're parents, that we should be on a diet, that we should keep an immaculate house, that we should work in the yard to maintain a perfect lawn, that we should be actively involved in extracurricular activities, and on and on. Hundreds of years ago, Native Americans lived free and spiritual lives and only did the things they wanted to do. The word *should* wasn't even part of their language. In our contemporary culture, the word *should* is used to control us.

Our time is filled up with a vast number of things we don't really want to do. I can't tell you how many people I've worked with who make hundreds of thousands of dollars but feel guilty because they don't mow the lawn or wash the car. Many people are not comfortable unless they are constantly busy. This mindset of speed and endless rushing about is a huge cultural trap. Throughout Part Two, I'll be sharing some simple ways to help you simplify your life and live in sync with time.

Hiring a Personal Assistant

We perform many of the activities in our lives because we believe we "should" be doing them, but they don't add meaning to our lives. Some of these activities we can simply dispense with, as we'll explore more fully in subsequent chapters. We can easily pay someone else to do many of the rest.

What I'm about to say is very important: if you do not like certain chores, you can hire someone else to do them! Depending on your salary, you can work one hour per day, per week, or per month doing something you love, and use what you earn to pay someone to do what you don't like to do. Personal assistants are part-time or full-time employees who are administrators for your personal household. I always describe this position to a new personal assistant as follows: "Your job is to keep me free to work [practice my profession] and play." Personal assistants are usually college graduates who work hard and are smart and very committed.

When I was a busy lawyer, I hired a personal assistant whom I paid really well to do the things I didn't like to do. I'd write down the things I liked to do, and the personal assistant's job was to do everything else, such as shining my shoes, pressing my clothes, and, if I felt like cooking, getting the ingredients ready for me. After working eight hours, I'd arrive home and everything would be done. Even though I'm not that busy today, I continue to employ a personal assistant.

You can always instruct a personal assistant to leave some things for you to do that you genuinely enjoy, such as thirty minutes of yard work or ironing or the final stages of preparing a fine meal. When you employ a personal assistant, you and your partner will have time to sit down and talk to each other and plan other adventures in your lives. Remember, you can almost always hire someone else to perform the tasks you don't like doing yourself. This will allow you to rearrange the time you have so that you can enjoy each moment to the maximum.

Being in the Moment

People often ask me, "How can I live in the moment?" That's not really the question. If it were, the answer would be "You don't have any other choice!" What people are really asking with this question is, "How can I be aware of and appreciate each moment of my life?" When we ask this question, we are opening the door to a deeper understanding of coming into integrity with time.

We live our lives as a seemingly infinite series of split seconds. During each split second, everything in the universe, including most aspects of ourselves, are exactly how they are, and there is nothing we can change. The one small aspect of ourselves that we can change is our attitude toward the split second of time. Our capacity to choose our attitude holds the key to coming into integrity in our relationship with time. If we are worrying, if we are projecting ourselves into the future, if we are yearning for the past, or if we are fearful or hopeful, we aren't appreciating the moment. If we are resisting anything in our lives that we can't or won't change, we are out of integrity with this split second of our lives. If, in this split second, we are trying to change things we cannot change, not accepting what we can't change, or ignoring the numerous possibilities of each moment, we do not have integrity with time.

Many people worry or agonize over things that have occurred or that might occur in their lives. They hold onto anger against people who have hurt them in the past. This anger and worry keep them from being in the present moment. Such anger only hurts the person who carries it. The secret of being at peace with the drama in our lives is to learn to accept the unacceptable. When we resist what is, we are pulled out of the moment. If I catch myself falling into worrying or being angry about things I cannot change, I repeat to myself, "It is what it is" until I bring myself back into the moment.

People who follow the philosophy I'm promoting in *Time and Money* appreciate the gift of life. Each split second is a gift. If our attitude in each split second is dedicated to freedom, independence, and self-integrity in a context of sanctuary (a place of safety) empowered by love, our lives have a continuous flow of meaning. Some people are very persnickety and finicky regarding the kind of split second they are willing to find meaningful. For instance, they might find work, sex, golfing, or eating more meaningful than washing the dishes, ironing, or waiting in line. In my experience, such people become increasingly pickier with regard to which split seconds they will enjoy, until finally they don't enjoy any split seconds at all. As I keep adjusting my attitude to come closer to total integrity with time, I find meaning in an increasing percentage of the split seconds of my life. I feel fulfilled. Coming into this kind of integrity with time is the key to living in the moment.

CHAPTER 19

Living in Sync with Time

In this chapter we'll look at some of the basic principles for bringing your life into sync with time, which is the same as being in integrity with time moment by moment.

The Extremes of Rushing and Slowing Down

When it comes to time, too often we try to rush into the future and speed time up by working faster. This doesn't work, and it creates great anxiety and frustration. If you're rushing through work because you want to have more money, instead consider raising your prices, getting a different job, or reducing your spending and slowing down some. If you want to live in the present, then take some things out of your schedule! All of your rushing around pushes you out of the present and into the future. This isn't comfortable; in fact, it's often just plain unpleasant. We're trying to rush through our lives rather than truly live them!

We even schedule our children with so many activities that they have no free time for exploration or adventure. In this way, we're teaching them to be anxious about time, too. We're all aware of how much our society has speeded up over the last century. Over the next hundred years, our society will speed up another hundred times! No wonder we have so many antianxiety drugs. It is amazing we can even function.

At the other extreme, when people say they are bored, this is usually a signal that they are out of sync with time in the opposite direction. What they have done is slow down too much. We can slow down so much that we find ourselves swept up in worry, nostalgia, or regret. This is the equivalent of being pulled out of the present and into the past. In children, slowing down too much is called boredom, but in adults it is usually called depression. It tends to be dispiriting, and it's no way to live life.

Getting Back in Sync with Time

As we've just seen, there are two ways to be out of sync with time. One is trying to speed time up and push into the future, and the opposite is slowing down too much and being dragged into the past. Both of these states are stressful. When we start freeing up our time, we have more choices. Sometimes we have too many choices, and this can feel confusing and overwhelming. It can lead to a slight depression or a scattered feeling and a sense that we don't know what to do first. When this occurs, first relax and sit on a park bench until you decide what you really want to do. Then focus on one thing you love doing and expand it to the right amount of time. This activity could be reading, writing, gourmet cooking, photography, painting, or traveling—the list goes on.

Instead of living to get through the day, try living for the enjoyment of the activity you are doing at the moment. I always make positive decisions with my time and never take on more during a day than feels right with my integrity with time. I only do the things that are meaningful to me, and I never do what I "should" do. There seem to be two kinds of people in the world: those who do what they most want to do first, and those who do what they least want to do first. Some eat their favorite jellybeans first, while others eat their favorites last. One way to live well is to do the things we really want to do *first*. A true respect for time means we do *only* what we want to do.

Perhaps it's time to start rearranging your life and gearing it for your normal brain capacity, which is slower than the pace at which so many of us are rushing around. What I particularly like about traveling or unstructured exploring is that I am just dealing with things as they come up. I'm not locked into time. I really enjoy the type of vacation where my partner Lori and I just get into our car and drive, not knowing where we are going to end up. This is an example of getting in sync with time because there is no place to go, no time to get there, and nothing you *have* to do once you arrive. Keeping this image in mind can serve to remind you how to live in sync with time. If you're experiencing anxiety and tension, these are signs that you're not in integrity with time.

The Success and Failure Myth

The noted writer Joseph Campbell was a college professor who taught and wrote about cultural myths. Cultural myths are stories about humanity and our world. Every culture creates its own story and then acts it out. The cultural myth predominant in the United States stresses that the end result is what counts, not enjoying the process of getting to that result. Many of the stories we remember from childhood, such as the stories of Snow White and Cinderella, reflect this. In these stories, the main characters endure difficult lives but live "happily ever after." The final line of the story is presented as justifying the agonizing process that led up to it.

In our culture, this story line has been amplified into the myth of success and failure. What do we ask Little Leaguers when they come home from the game? "Did you win?" We don't ask them what it felt like to swing the bat or catch the ball. Another question adults ask children all the time is "What do you want to be when you grow up?" This is such a future-oriented question, focused on a goal or end result, rather than on the present, moment-by-moment reality of a child's life. In addition, we encourage children to strive for good grades rather than simply experience the fun of learning. Many people who got straight A's will tell you later that they did not learn all that much and that it was not much fun. It's important to distinguish between symbols and end results, such as grades or the score at the end of a game, and the actual process and experience. Many times we do not enjoy the process because we are focused on the end result and the symbol that goes along with it. When you are living in the process itself, you become more present in what you're doing. Your life expands and grows longer and longer.

There are a few basic problems with striving for success and avoiding failure. Generally, you can only tell whether something is a success or failure after it is over. We also need to have the agreement of other people for the symbols of success or failure to have any meaning. Let's say we are watching a football game and enjoying it; we have to wait until the game is over to get to the symbol or the score. This is a short process compared to a marriage, which can last many years. How will I know if my marriage has been successful? Will it be at the time of my death or divorce? Life is the longest process we go through, and we will only know if it has been "successful" when we die! Does this make any sense? If I live my life for the current cultural symbols of success or failure, I can't know if my life is a success until it is over. How many people in this culture would settle for a great epitaph on their grave marker or a well-written obituary?

When we don't know the end result but are attached to the symbols of success, quite often we find ourselves anxious and not enjoying the process. Anxiety in a football game may translate into excitement, but anxiety in a marriage or a life is usually called *stress.*

Remember, the reason we look outside ourselves for validation is that we need to have the agreement of other people for our symbols to have any meaning. As you've heard me say before, life is a process, not an end; if you don't enjoy the process, you're going to hate the end! This principle applies to a great many areas, such as parenting, relationships, marriage, learning, preparing a meal, and vacations. We'll be happier when we shift our attention to the process, not the end.

Symbols of success aren't just grades or game scores. Here's a list of some of our culture's symbols of success:

Having a fancy car or a big truck

Having a big house

Having plenty of money

Wearing an expensive watch or jewelry

Sending our kids to private schools

Having a college degree

Having articles or books published

Owning a second home

Taking elaborate vacations

Owning a boat

Having a well-stocked wine cellar

Public recognition, such as getting our name in the paper

Having well-behaved and successful children

Gourmet dining

Having a maid

Shopping at high-end stores

Being able to retire early

Having a platinum Visa card

Owning a successful business

Getting good grades

Having a large investment portfolio

Living in the "right" neighborhood

Associating with famous people

Having enough to be philanthropic

Winning awards and trophies

Having a trophy husband or wife

Owning expensive art

Some symbols of failure as it is currently defined by our culture (or as it has recently been defined by our culture; these symbols are constantly shifting and evolving) include:

Getting divorced

Having to declare bankruptcy

Having a "problem child"

Not owning jewelry

Committing suicide

Being addicted to a drug or alcohol

Living in poverty

Being fired

Being charged with malpractice

Being sued

Having poor health or a mental illness

Being unhappy

Having no pension

Having something repossessed

Having no friends

Going to jail

Being in debt

Being unemployed

Being childless

Being homeless

Not having a spouse or partner

Being on welfare

Being homosexual

Having AIDS

Being single

Note that none of the symbols I've listed for either success or failure has an absolute relationship to happiness. You might like some of them and not like others, but the bottom line is that it's possible to be happy or unhappy no matter how many items you can check off on either or both lists. All of these trappings of success or failure simply aren't the point. As the character played by Bill Murray in the movie *Meatballs* so wisely stated, "It just doesn't matter."

Eliminating Clutter

When we are speeding around trying to fit too much into too little time in an attempt to amass the cultural symbols of success, it becomes impossible to truly enjoy life. We need to learn to say no without guilt, and never waste energy on justifying or explaining ourselves. Eliminating the time clutter in our lives frees us up to come into sync with time.

Another way to be in integrity with time is to do what we need to do instead of putting it off and wasting time worrying and thinking about it, which is a form of mental clutter. It is possible to do what we want, at the speed we want, all the time. Worrying and resistance pull us out of time; there is no present action or result in worrying. When I intuitively feel that I don't want to do something, I don't do it. I sense when the time is right to do something, and I don't worry about it beforehand.

I also make sure to schedule time to do the things that I really want to do. I eliminate all of the clutter in my house and at work. I never take work home. I've found that never taking work home has been one of the greatest gifts I have given my family.

Watching TV or playing computer games can be a waste of time, but it can also be a time of relaxation just for you. If you are watching TV or playing games compulsively, this may be a form of avoidance, but if you're genuinely relaxing and making time less important with these activities, that's great. This is enjoying your life. Learning to distinguish between time clutter and relaxation is part of the process.

Being Irresponsible

If I deleted wasted time from your schedule, you would have plenty of time left over for all that is meaningful to you. I have virtually no time clutter in my life. When I recognize it, I get rid of it immediately. I do not see people I don't feel bonded with. I don't join clubs, and I do only what I want to do. As a result of this, I am totally irresponsible. *Responsibility* is a near sacred word in the English language; it means doing something you don't want to do because you "should" do it. I don't do *anything* I don't want to do. Sometimes people tell me I look like a very responsible person, but this is a total illusion.

Using the word *procrastination* is a way of beating yourself up for not doing something you don't want to do. How do you know what you want to do when you're so used to doing what you "should" do? You give yourself permission to quit doing the things you don't want to do! I have done this many times. When I was a young lawyer seeing sixteen clients a day, one day I got up and said to myself, "I don't feel like going to work." I had eight clients scheduled that morning, but I took off my coat, unbuttoned my shirt, and made myself another cup of coffee. I sat there savoring my coffee for about fifteen minutes until I could genuinely hardly wait to get into the office to see my clients. This experience made me realize that I *wanted* to go to work. Once I gave myself permission *not* to go to work, I found that my energy and performance increased dramatically. I got so good at doing this that eventually I would take three months off at a time. When I got back from my adventures, I would be ready to go to work again out of pure choice, without a trace of obligation.

Some people feel a duty to spend time with certain people or get together with relatives they don't even like. This is a real waste of time. It lacks integrity. If I invited you to my house but you did not want to come and came anyway, I would be insulted because this lacks self-integrity. If you don't want to be there with an acquaintance or relatives, I guarantee they don't want to be there, either. I'll be guiding you through clearing the clutter out of your life in subsequent chapters.

Many type-A action-oriented people have a delusion that they are not in control of their time; of course, they are actually in total control of every minute. We have a choice about every second of our lives. We have all the time we need to live full and beautiful lives. It is time to eliminate the things that keep us in a rut of feeling trapped by obligations.

If you knew you were going to die today, you would create twenty-four hours of free time. One choice is to die and get twenty-four hours of free time; the other choice is not to die, acknowledge that you're in control of your time, make skillful choices about your time on a minute-to-minute basis, and live a fulfilled life.

Capturing Time

What I call *captured time* is usually the most meaningful time of our lives. Let me give you an example of what I mean by captured time. When the great artist Michelangelo created the sculpture of David, he took about two years to do it, and he loved every minute of it. Some five hundred years later, this magnificent sculpture is Michelangelo's captured time. When I look at the house that my partner Lori and I created over a couple of years, I know it is my captured time and will be here five hundred years from now. When I create a seminar, that, too, is captured time; it lives on in the people who attend the seminar. Doing the things I really love, taking the time to use my artistic and creative ability—all this becomes captured time.

Most of time we spend is fleeting. It disappears. It is intangible. When I think of the time I went on a three-month sailing trip with my children, Amy and Kyle, I remember when my back was burned and eight-year-old Amy lovingly peeled off the dead skin. This is captured, meaningful time for me. So much of our busy-as-a-bee time just disappears and is meaningless to us. What are the times you can look back on that have added richness to your life? What did you create? What did you imagine? What experiences did you have? I would like you to look at each moment of time in this way. As we simplify our lives, we are actually doing more of what we want to do.

Doing What We Want to Do

The ideal for the rest of our lives is to do only what we want to do. At the end of their lives, most people wish they had done more of the things they wanted to do; they certainly don't wish they could do more of what they didn't want to do! There is no good reason for not doing what we want and for living our dreams fully and completely. Our lives are so much more joyful when we're not doing anything we don't want to do. To come into sync with time, stop filling it with things you "should" do and instead do only what you truly want to do!

When you truly live your beautiful life story, it may look to others as if you are being responsible. That's okay, so long as you are clear inside yourself that you are totally irresponsible—that is, that you are coming from your own integrity, not someone else's expectations.

If we are totally irresponsible, we can be free and independent, and we can practice total self-integrity in sync with time.

CHAPTER 20

Clearing Out the Junk

We can safely assume that time cannot be changed and, as I stated earlier, we cannot make more time or save time. In this chapter, we'll explore the ways our lives may not fit time and look at how we can move toward a relationship with time marked by integrity.

Identifying Junk

Junk is anything that does not add meaning to our lives. Junk can be a second house, an old car, gold or silver hidden away somewhere, or anything else that does not add meaning to our lives. Because we have rationalized so much of our junk, we are unaware that it exists. Nonetheless, our houses are full of junk. Our lives are full of junk. There is material junk, there is time junk, there is conceptual junk, and there is possession junk. Imagine going into each of your closets and storage areas and looking at every item and asking, "Does this add meaning to my life?" As a rule, if something doesn't add meaning to your life, get rid of it.

I usually go through my ties every couple of months and get rid of the ones that don't add meaning to my life. In one closet I once found forty shirts; I realized that these were my painting shirts, and I don't even paint! I gave these shirts to the painter who was touching up my house. I think I saw him wearing one at a restaurant; they were pretty good painting shirts. Some people will even pay you for your junk; just go on eBay and take a look at what's offered! My son, Kyle, has an interesting approach. Around Halloween he puts his junk out in the yard and tells the trick-or-treaters to take whatever they want. One year I saw a chunky boy grab a TV set that still worked and hurry home. Other people want your junk!

We get used to having junk around, and we don't realize how much it drains our energy. Every time we open a closet and see the clothing we haven't worn for years, it is psychologically draining. This is particularly true with exercise equipment that we're not using; seeing it tends to makes us feel guilty. When possessions stop adding meaning to your life, it's time to sell them or give them away. If you later find you need that possession, you can always buy it again. If you follow the *Time and Money* game plan for economic freedom you learned in Part One, you will have plenty of money to buy anything again if you want it.

Here are some examples of large junk:

A rental property

A boat

A second car

A time-share apartment

An exercise machine

Holding on to such junk long after it has ceased to have any meaning in your life is not only emotionally draining, it is financially draining because you have to insure it, store it, clean it, and worry about it. Some people pay a storage facility huge amounts of money to store their junk; very few of these people could even tell you what is in their storage area!

I find that owning a house adds meaning to my life. Right now, I also find that owning a vacation house adds meaning to my life. Aside from these two houses, no other real estate would add meaning to my life.

Magazines and professional journals can be draining; if you have not read them in five days, throw them out. If something is worth reading, it is worth reading today. Develop systems for clearing out your junk on a regular basis. It is amazing how many people keep receipts and other papers. If your parents taught you to be a pack rat, it is time to quit. Be very diligent in getting rid of the junk in your life. Test all of your possessions to see if they add meaning to your life. This puts you in control of them and prevents them from controlling you. Wouldn't it be great to only have things in your life that add meaning? Exercise 9 in Appendix A will help you identify and get rid of the junk in your life.

Identifying Time Junk

It is good to have quiet time, but it is also important to have the time to put our energy into the fun things that we want to do with power and gusto. Simplifying our lives and clearing out the clutter is really about creating more power. Create a list of things that add meaning to your life and amplify your life story. Now do the things that are on top of your list. As children, we were compelled to do things that we did not want to do, but as adults we no longer have to feel that way. It is a compulsion that does not feel good.

Along with physical junk, our lives are too often cluttered with organizational junk, such as belonging to committees that do not add meaning to our lives. Joining clubs and committees that are not meaningful is a big waste of time. At one point these activities may have added meaning to your life, but if they no longer do, it's time to quit doing them.

Here are some examples of areas where your life may not be fitting time:

Rushing home from work

Having deadlines

Rushing to the airport

Exercising quickly

Participating in children's extracurricular activities

Having children with lists of things to do

Having lengthy telephone conversations

Eating fast foods

Having lengthy lists of things to do

Being on hold

Waiting in line

Doing the dishes

Getting slowed down in traffic or construction zones

Dealing with contractors

Gathering information or dealing with information overload

Surfing the Internet

Staying caught up with email and other correspondence

Staying current with journals, magazines, or newspapers

Serving on committees or belonging to organizations

Dreading the alarm clock

Paying bills

Putting too much on your plate

Saying yes

Agreeing to do things when you don't have enough time

Volunteering

Dealing with junk mail

Reviewing legal contracts

Justifying and explaining

Watching TV or playing video games

Dealing with computers

Experiencing procrastination or other forms of resistance

Worrying

There are so many ways that our modern lives have gotten out of sync with time. One trap that pulls us out of sync with time is saying yes or agreeing to do things when we don't have enough time to do them. Take a look at your time junk and eliminate anything that isn't meaningful. Exercise 10 in Appendix A helps you evaluate how to spend your time, and Exercise 11 helps you explore the roles you take on and other aspects of your relationship with yourself.

Here are some changes you can make in your life to rid yourself of time clutter and come into greater sync with time:

Let go of roles that no longer fit you.

Say no.

Quit or do not join organizations.

Hire help and delegate less meaningful tasks.

Eliminate "shoulds."

Follow your feelings.

Make conscious choices.

Do not buy into family pressures.

Plan better.

Buy and drive the fun car.

Don't answer until you know.

Simplify.

Eliminate junk and things you're doing that you don't want to do.

Only talk with people you want to talk with.

Only be with people you want to be with.

Get rid of the cell phone.

Don't worry about running late.

Don't make excuses.

Go to more baseball games.

Make sure you schedule time for the things you want to do.

Never take work home.

When we rid ourselves of time junk—activities or roles that take up time without adding meaning to our lives—we reclaim our freedom.

Clearing Out Social Junk

It's also important to get rid of social junk, which means being involved with people who do not add meaning to our lives. Sometimes we have known people for years, and we feel obligated to do things with them even though we would rather be doing something else. Sometimes relationships from the past have fallen to the wayside, but we still feel an obligation to keep them alive. Even though these relationships clutter our lives and rob us of our time, it can be hard to drop them for fear of rejection or being alone. I assure you that it is always better to be in the present with your relationships.

In order to simplify your life, focus on a few close relationships and give yourself the opportunity to enjoy quality interactions with these people. From now on, decide to spend time only with the people who add meaning to your life because they give you energy and joy and you feel fulfilled around them.

Many of us belong to clubs and organizations for the wrong reasons. Serving on committees can be a great time waster that doesn't add meaning to our lives. Holidays such as Christmas or Passover can become anxiety-ridden and extremely stressful, especially if we feel we have to make them perfect. These special days are meant to be times of joy and happiness, but most of what I see is stress and anxiety, except at our house, where we've successfully recaptured the fun.

Here are some examples of social junk:

Seeing people we don't want to see

Staying tied in to family obligations

Stressing ourselves preparing for holidays or other social gatherings

Maintaining friendships long after any common interest has faded away

Corresponding by letter or email with people we don't like

Spending time in groups that aren't meaningful to us

Many times, our relationships with our siblings or parents can be very stressful. I have found that "blood" is not "thicker than water." It is more important to be around family members we enjoy and to let go of those we don't. If you really don't want to see someone, you know this on a gut level. Give yourself permission to quit seeing people who give you an anxious feeling in the pit of your stomach. Then check to see how it feels not to see them. If you choose not to see a certain family member, then set a context so that others in your family can better understand your decision. For example, you could tell your mother that it would be lying to pretend you enjoy being with your brother-in-law because it is not true for you; when you are with your brother-in-law, it violates your integrity. If you do like seeing your sister, you can always meet her away from her husband.

The first thing you need to do is to get clear. The way you get clear is to give yourself permission not to be with people when it doesn't feel meaningful. Once you do this, honesty comes more easily. I know that if I don't like being with people, they probably don't like being with me. When human beings come together, they know how other people feel. Once one person is honest, everybody else has permission to be honest. There are people on this planet who are just not particularly interesting to me. This doesn't necessarily mean I dislike them; I simply choose not to spend time with them. For example, I find righteous people boring because they always think they are right. If you are caught in negative relationships with people who have qualities you actively do not like, this is probably a reflection of something in yourself. Once you accept that quality in them, you are more likely to be able to accept it in yourself. When we see people we don't want to see, we are really lying and giving up our integrity. Telling the truth to ourselves is what sets us free. Exercise 12 in Appendix A will help you explore your relationship with others and clear out the social junk that keeps you from being in sync with time. Either let go of the relationships that don't add meaning to your life or change the context so they do add meaning.

CHAPTER 21

Simplifying Your Life

As we grow older, our lives seem to become increasingly more complex. We have paperwork to stay on top of, investments to keep track of, records to keep, taxes to file. This complexity permeates every aspect of our lives and dampens our effectiveness, our peace of mind, and our very aliveness. Our culture explicitly teaches us that greatness is obtained in ways that complicate our lives. We're taught to consume, consume, consume, yet most of the objects we obtain make our lives more complicated, not less. If we are looking for a life that is powerful, effective, loving, joyous, and peaceful, we'll probably find it 180 degrees away from cultural norms. We need to harness the incredible power of simplicity. Most of us disseminate our aliveness into an unbelievable array of objects, people, ideas, places, organizations, hobbies, and materialism. The more we add, the less effective we become.

It is helpful to observe young children from four to six years old playing without adult supervision. Observe the power and unburdened aliveness present in the children's activities. All of their energy goes into what they're doing in the moment. Children's lives are already simplified so that they focus fully on the act they're engaging in. Feel the power of simplicity in your observation.

Cultivating Simplicity

The moment we form an intent and act on that intent, we experience the power of simplicity. Every act of simplification adds potency and power to our lives. If you did Exercise 9 in Appendix A, you have already listed every object large and small that you own. You have asked whether each item is meaningful to your life. If you found the answer was yes, then for now you are keeping the item. If your answer was no, did you follow through by immediately selling, donating, or giving away the object? This followthrough is the key to living with simplicity. The money you earn from selling these objects gives you stored power and adds flexibility and choice.

Then, in Exercise 10, you carefully listed how you spend your time. If you listed every activity, from those taking seconds to those taking hours or days, and then asked whether these time expenditures add meaning to your life, you have begun the process. Did you follow through by beginning to eliminate or delegate those activities that don't add meaning?

Next, in Exercise 11 and Exercise 12, you moved your focus to relationships. You listed all of the people in your life— family, friends, relatives, and acquaintances. You asked whether the time you spend with them adds meaning to your life. If your answer was no, have you begun the process of letting go of these relationships or reinventing the context?

It's so important to simplify. Personal and physical simplicity involves examining how you dress, groom, eat, and exercise and moving in the direction of greater ease and less complication.

Once you've gotten rid of your physical junk, your time junk, and your social junk, you can now shift your focus to spiritual simplicity. Spiritual simplicity means following one simple philosophy: your own. It means looking inside yourself, not outside yourself, for your truth. My code is to live a life of freedom, independence, and self-integrity in a context of sanctuary, empowered by unburdened aliveness on a bedrock of truth.

Simplicity and Creativity

Make a conscious practice of eliminating all of the things you do by habit or by custom that don't add meaning to your life. You cannot be creative when your life is too complex. All creativity arises from simplicity. All the great people in world history, from Leonardo da Vinci to Claude Monet, understood the power of simplicity; they were focused on what was meaningful in their lives. They scheduled time to relax and to allow creativity to emerge.

When you simplify your life, you feel lighter. All the things you think you have to do feel very heavy. In essence, all you need to do to simplify your life is to eliminate the things that feel heavy. Remember what you have learned about the power of simplicity by watching young children at play. For children, everything is immediate; they only concentrate on the present. Children tend to bubble with creativity because they are living in the present.

Perhaps you can remember a time in your life when things were very simple and joyous. When I was a freshman in high school, I looked forward to a summer with nothing to do. I remember how light and excited I felt when I walked out of school because I had no agenda. It was one of the greatest summers of my life; I went to the beach and didn't have plans about what I was going to do from day to day.

Have you ever had times like that in your life? It is important to remember such times, because your life can still be that way. If you can feel it, you can bring it back.

Of course, some of you will say you never had unstructured, free-spirited time in your childhood, perhaps because your type-A parents have kept you busy ever since you were born. Even so, it's never too late to give yourself the gift of unstructured time. If you're feeling a creative block, be sure to set aside some simple, unstructured time as soon as possible.

Enjoying Simplicity

Another time I remember fondly is when I got my first apartment and there was nothing in it. I had so much fun decorating it simply, with a fruit box for a nightstand. It was so much fun to fix the place up with the simplest of accessories. One of the keys to simplicity is that you cannot make choices until you free some space by ridding yourself of choices you have already made. Making room for new choices gives us a true sense of freedom.

Another simple time in my life was when I crossed the ocean. I was just in the present. Everything was so beautiful, I did not want to find land. There was a good chance I wasn't going to, because I was learning navigation on the way! The only thing I had to deal with was what was happening at the moment. I was sailing, eating, or fishing, and everything was light and easy. I'll tell you the full story of that memorable trip in Chapter 24.

I loved the story of Robinson Crusoe as a child. When Crusoe landed on the island, he got rid of society. The novel *Robinson Crusoe* is based on a true story. We, too, are able to re-create our lives out of new possibilities, but we do not have to go to the extreme of a Robinson Crusoe to simplify our lives. In this book, I've been giving you the tools to help you simplify and see what really is important. And if everything you are doing now already adds meaning to your life and you're never plagued with anxiety or stress, you have already done it! Now you can simply enjoy every single moment of your life.

CHAPTER 22

Simplifying Your Family's Life

Most of us spend a great deal of time on insignificant tasks that do not add meaning to our lives, but we feel guilty if we do not do them. Some parents feel guilty because they think it is important for their kids to see them mopping the floor, mowing the lawn, and doing all of this drudgery so that they will learn to do this kind of stuff themselves. A better idea is to have someone else perform these tasks so that you're fresh and can spend three hours of quality time with your children. As your quality of life improves, your children will realize that it's possible to earn a living doing what they love and that drudgery does not have to be part of life. You'll also have more time to spend with your spouse or partner.

Family Imprinting about Time

In this culture, we've adopted a crazy perspective about time. Many people don't think they have enough time. If we came to our senses, we would realize that we have all the time we need to do everything we want in our lives. When we are rushed, we cannot be creative so we don't have time to think about doing something new.

All of us have received unhealthy imprinting with regard to time. Here are some of the phrases that reflect the family imprinting that teaches us that if we're not busy, there must be something wrong with us:

Free time is bad time.

It has to be hard to be good.

Don't waste time.

Don't be late.

Time is money.

Time is love.

Earn your way every day.

Don't be lazy.

A rolling stone gathers no moss.

Be busy as a bee.

Busy hands are happy hands.

Can't you find something to do?

We are trained as children to be on time for school, on time with our homework, on time for sports events, and so on; even as children, all too often we run from one thing to another. Today, children are even more heavily scheduled; there are children only six years old whose schedules are already so full they are burdened with stress and anxiety! Do all of these activities truly add meaning to our children's lives?

Time and Relationships

One of the important elements for healthy relationships is time. This doesn't mean we have to be together all the time. Many women just want to talk and be listened to, but many men think they don't have the time to talk so they just give curt answers. Many children just want us to spend unstructured time with them, but many parents don't find the time just to be with their children and instead park them in front of the television or computer as some kind of electronic babysitter.

Part of any healthy conversation is spending time to listen. When my partner Lori raises an emotional issue, I know she is not doing it to complain but to communicate. When I take the time to listen, our relationship deepens.

Most relationships are not that happy because we just do not make time for them. Simplify your life and your family's life so that you have meaningful time to enjoy life together! Do Exercise 13 in Appendix A, and watch your family relationships thrive.

CHAPTER 23

Creating and Enjoying New Experiences

As I pointed out earlier, as people get older, they often think their lives are speeding by because they're on automatic. When you're busy every single second and are stuck in a routine, your life goes by so quickly you do not even know you have lived. My life is getting longer because I know how to deliberately create a longer life. If you go on vacation to a place you have never been before, the first part of the vacation seems really long, and then it begins to speed up toward the end. This is because you are already getting used to it, and as it becomes a habit, you start taking things for granted. This is when your life starts to disappear. Our experience of time is more about perspective and less about the passing hours on a clock.

Breaking Out of the Rut

It's important to give yourself plenty of opportunities to go off automatic and throw yourself into different circumstances in life. While you can do this in any setting, sometimes it helps to travel somewhere completely new. I remember some years ago when Lori and I took a trip to Japan. Everything was new to us. Turning on a light switch was different, the plumbing was different, meeting people was different. The whole experience was like a gigantic and fun lesson on perspective.

Though it can sometimes be intense, we all have the opportunity to go off automatic and throw ourselves into different circumstances no matter where we find ourselves. We can practice new behaviors and activities on a daily basis in both our personal and work environments. For the rest of our lives, we can create thousands of new experiences instead of trying to make our lives ordinary or usual or stereotypically "peaceful." When we move to a new town, the first five or six months often feel like five years because of all of the new opportunities and experiences.

We all have the opportunity to experience this phenomenon every day of our lives. Instead of doing easy or automatic things, we can keep pushing ourselves into new learning and new experiences. If we challenge ourselves every single day and keep seeking new opportunities in everything we do, our lives expand instead of contract. In this way, we can be like Methuselah, who, if you'll recall, is said to have lived to the ripe old age of 969. If we are discovering new things every day and cultivating a willingness to look at the parts of life we tend to resist, we'll find that these are the parts that will lengthen our lives. When we challenge ourselves every single day to take on new adventures and challenges instead of doing the same old thing, our experience of life deepens immeasurably. And remember, some of the biggest challenges may actually reside in shifting the smallest of habits in favor of something new. We have a tendency to see our lives, relationships, and/or our jobs in terms of the broad strokes instead of the detail of the small brush strokes. The true adventure of our lives resides in the details. This is a bit like looking at a painting by Vincent van Gogh or another master. Each little brush stroke makes up the canvas of the painting. Each little detail forms the fabric of our lives. We are taught to live for major events, instead of for the details. But by doing this, we lose our lives. In contrast, our lives can be filled with incredible beauty and a multitude of gifts if we just start paying attention to the details.

Paying Attention to the Small Details

Indeed, much of the joy and happiness we find in life comes from paying attention to and appreciating the details, whether in the form of a beautiful sunset, flowers blooming, or other gifts we are given. I used to own a beach house on the ocean. I remember early one morning I made myself a cup of coffee and went out to sit on a sofa outdoors. At first it was pitch black. Then, as it started to get lighter, I noticed a little red streak in the sky and the fog close to the shore. The water was almost placid, and as I watched, a big dolphin leaped out of the water, followed by other dolphins. As I watched the dolphins cut through the water, some pelicans came in and started diving in front of them. I was given such a beautiful gift that morning, and it was taking the time to pay attention to the details that allowed me to receive it.

Virtually every day I start my day slow. I get up early and take about an hour for quiet and peace. This helps me get the rest of the day in sync by reminding me that there's nothing to rush about. Each day I create as many new experiences and adventures as possible. We go to new places all the time; we try different things on the menu. We start to pay attention to new experiences instead of staying in the same old rut. Living in a rut is like putting our feet on the accelerator of time; life rushes by like a blur of passing scenery we're moving too fast to appreciate. Time offers the perspective on how much I am living. Every time I read a new book, do something different, or take on a new challenge, this lengthens my life. I took up gourmet cooking to add more variety. I love to listen to books on tapes, and I enjoy my pugs. Lori and I sometimes just get in the car and travel for a week without any agenda or a place to go. At the beginning of the year, we block out time on our calendars for trips or simply for time for ourselves.

Taking Time Off

When I was a busy lawyer, every three or four years I would take three months off, which most people are afraid to do. In a key respect, my decision to take that large a chunk of time off had to do with passing through the illusion of fear and choosing not to limit myself. Whenever I have gone through fear and reached the other side, I've experienced a remarkable shift in the way I see things. Contrast is the essence of vision; when we do something that is in total contrast to what we do every day, we experience life afresh upon our return.

In 1974 I left my practice for my three months off. I sailed with my wife and children, who were six and eight at the time, up to Desolation Sound in British Columbia. This area is absolutely beautiful. There are fantastic totem poles and colorful small villages. Taking this long trip marked a big transition in my life. We were so remote that when we left Nixon was president, and when we got back, he wasn't.

From then on, whenever I took my three months off, I would go to some remote place and never call home. I found that one of the greatest things to do is to seemingly slip out of planet Earth and walk away from all the things I thought I had to do. Most of us fall into a pattern of thinking our usual routine is important, but when we drop out of it we find we have plenty of time and yet the world goes on. There's nothing that lengthens life more than taking time off. When life is complex, time flies; when we simplify, we create longer lives. I've decided to live forever, so I keep simplifying—and enjoying!

CHAPTER 24

Enjoying the Adventure of Life

Significant truths are often best conveyed through stories. In this chapter, I'm going to share an important story from my life with you. At first it may seem like just a nice story, but don't be fooled. This simple story contains everything you need to know to be successful in business and life.

In the summer of 1979, I decided to take another three months off to sail to Hawaii with Gina, my girlfriend at the time. The trip turned out to be a major catalyst in my life. The thought of crossing the ocean terrified me. My fear was simple: I was afraid of getting lost. I had never before sailed out of easy reach of land. Crossing the ocean meant I would have to learn to navigate with a sextant, and that entailed paying attention to a great many details. In those days, there were no electronic navigation systems available. I hated details, especially mathematical details. I was extremely busy trying to get everything done before I left, and I had little time to learn navigation. A few months before I left, I bought a Westsail 43, which is one of the finest boats built for heavy weather. If I were going to die, I wanted it to be my fault, not the boat's! I equipped the boat with three years' worth of supplies, so that if I didn't navigate very well I would probably hit land in that time. I bought two copies of the little blue book called *Navigation Made Easy* in case I dropped one overboard. I bought two sextants for the same reason. But the farther away from land we got, the less nervous and the more peaceful I became. By the time I learned how to navigate, I was way off course. The boat was far from any shipping lane, and we were really alone. For the first fifteen days, I saw only one ship.

During the daytime, I steered. For steering at night, I set up the wind vane, which was a small sail connected to the rudder. With wind vane steering, you can set the boat on course and as long as the wind stays the same, you'll be heading exactly the direction you have set. The problem is that you have to be aware of wind changes. At night I would go down and sleep for fifty-five minutes, then come up and check the direction to make sure the wind hadn't shifted and that we weren't going to be run down by another vessel. I'd go back and sleep for another fifty-five minutes and then get up again. I found I could do this instinctively without relying on an alarm clock, just on awareness.

A few days out, we hit a storm. I wasn't frightened by the storm at that point. I was just worried that it might get worse. As long as it stayed the way it was, I found it rather exciting. It started raining heavily after we left the Long Beach islands. The wind was blowing hard and continued to build up. After a few days, the waves were huge. I put the safety harness and lines on. I rigged the sails so I could handle them from the cockpit. Only the jib mainsail remained. I had taken one jib down and reefed the mainsail to the small triangle sail of the front jib. At the bottom of a wave, there was no wind. The wind continued to increase during the next five days of the storm. When we were in the middle of the waves, there was a wall of water in front of us and behind us. By the fourth and fifth days, the waves were even higher. As we chugged up the waves and got to the top, we would teeter and hope we weren't going to have to fall, but we knew we were. The boat would tip over, gather momentum, and plunge down about three stories, only to drive into the next wave and shudder to a stop. I tried to go straight into the waves ahead so we wouldn't breach. A wall of water would come back, and again we would start climbing. It was like going up the first part of a roller coaster.

Because of the clouds and the darkness, the water was dark green except for the white foam. I was a little frightened at first, but I became more excited as I got used to it. On the fifth day, at about three o'clock in the afternoon, the storm started to break. Rays of sun pierced through the clouds. I found myself at the back of the boat shooting down the gigantic waves yelling "Yippee!" as a wall of water would hit me when we crashed into each wave. My body was covered with salt. It was great! The next day the sky was clear blue and the sun was shining fully, even though the waves were still substantial. I felt really warm. Our forty-three-foot boat was like a postage stamp amidst the huge swells.

The next day the water became much calmer. The huge waves had settled down, and the sky was a clear and brilliant blue. The wind was blowing a gentle seven knots, and I looked up and saw that the sails of the boat were blowing full and the boat was riding smoothly through the water. I could hear the ripples of the bubbles along the hull. I have never been so at one with myself. I felt the best I had ever felt up to that moment in my life. The only evidence of the physical struggle of the previous five days was a deep, dark green swell, making the boat rise up and then race down. I felt a profound sense of peace. I loved it so much that I did not want to hit shore again. When you're sailing, you know when the storm's over and it's not going to get worse—it's only going to get better.

When those waters flattened and we started sailing again, it was such an incredible experience. I wish everybody could have it. You see that your whole world is like a circle no matter where you go. You realize that each day is all that counts, and you live for absolutely every moment. Every day is absolutely meaningful, and there is no future.

In an important moment after the storm, I came to realize a simple truth: I was alone. Gina was sick down below, and I experienced my profound aloneness. This awareness was fulfilling because it was so true. We are born alone, and we die alone. We live alone because we can't ever really be inside somebody else. This realization felt like the secret of life to me. The farther I got away from land, the more this feeling came over me. I realized I had been building up to this realization since I was a small child, and now it hit me like a tidal wave. In the past, when I was abandoned or hurt, I remembered being in great pain when I realized I was alone and would always be alone. Out on the water, I experienced a renewal of that feeling, only this time it was beautiful instead of painful.

This deep and peaceful knowing was as if God had spoken to me and revealed a fundamental piece of truth. I knew this realization was going to make a difference. It provided a key to how to see life. I had never felt anything like it before—a feeling of peace, of harmony, of quiet exaltation. I felt a freedom and an independence that I'd never experienced before, and yet it was mingled with a new feeling of being a part of the universe. I earned this new feeling and awareness by being uniquely myself with no compromises, regardless of what the world thought. As I sat there, I could feel the sun's rays gently caressing my shoulders. I felt at one with the sun.

As I looked around, I drank in the details I hadn't noticed fully before— the early morning sky, the dampness on the rails glistening in the sun, the long, deep green rolling swell that hinted of the chaos that had preceded it. The breeze, while fresh, seemed as gentle as a lamb as it caressed my face. Then I noticed that the boat was in a shambles. For the last seven days, I hadn't changed sails, coiled a rope, or done anything that was not absolutely necessary for survival. I didn't care because the joy inside me was so intense. I sang out to the universe, "I'm free. I'm free to go wherever I want, do whatever I want. Free to speak, to laugh, to shout, and to cry. I am free."

My body and clothes were caked with salt. I hadn't been able to undress for seven or eight days. First I took off my shirt, and it felt so good that I took off my pants, my socks, and my shorts. I stood up on the top of the deck and stretched and felt the warm rays of the sun and the cool touch of the breeze as they caressed my body. I noticed that I was covered with bruises. I had one pretty good cut, quite a few scratches, and several lumps. I reached up and tied the shower bag overhead. It had heated up through the sun's rays on the black plastic. I turned on the shower and washed all the salt off. I'd never had a shower that felt so good. I luxuriated in it. I turned it off and on. I soaped up and rinsed off again and again.

I began the slow process of shaving and combing my hair. I enjoyed every detail—even shaving, which usually seemed like such a bother. After I was finished, I lay on the deck, enjoying each moment of the morning. About an hour later, I went down into the cabin and began the process of putting on my best clothes. I picked my best pair of white shorts, my very best white

T-shirt. I enjoyed every aspect of dressing. I sat on the deck suffused with a sense of peace and love. I just loved everything; I loved the world, and I loved my life, and I loved the experience. It was so peaceful out at sea. I realized that my life was here and now. I didn't worry about anything elsewhere. I was living my life totally in the present. When I needed to fix the sails, I fixed the sails. And every moment I enjoyed the sun and the wind. It was just incredible to be in the present and to enjoy every aspect of life.

Now it was time to address the boat. I began the process of dousing the boat with water, scrubbing, coiling the ropes, taking down the storm sails and replacing them with the large light sails that would move the boat beautifully in this gentle wind. I put the winch in the socket and began the process of raising the mainsail. As it got higher and higher, I could feel the wind begin to push it over and drop a beautiful curve, an almost sculptured look, as the sail filled with a seven-knot breeze. I began the process of winching the jib. We heeled a little farther, and I felt the shudder of life go through the boat. I could feel the strength as the whole boat came alive and began the process of cutting through these long, slow rollers. It was like a bird fully alive flying across the water. I had a deep sense of satisfaction and wonder at being the master of this living thing.

I set the wind vane and turned my thoughts to breakfast. I was shocked to realize how famished I was. I was also surprised that I hadn't felt it until that moment. I checked the wind vane again, inspected the set of the sails, and adjusted the jib. Finally I was satisfied that I could attend to breakfast. I stepped down the wooden steps to the galley. I already knew what I was going to make: my favorite breakfast. I grated the potatoes, put on the bacon, and fried four extra large brown eggs I had bought from a farmer the week before we sailed. How good it smelled.

As I set the meal out in front of me, I felt profoundly grateful and again experienced the invigorating feeling of freedom and independence. I felt my unique self-truth come to me as I vociferously extinguished the hunger. I didn't know at the time that these feeling of freedom, independence, and self-integrity would never leave me. Something had changed permanently. I took a cup of coffee up on deck and sat in the sun. I looked at the sails and was well satisfied. The boat heeled beautifully and moved like an arrow through the water, rising up on one diminishing swell after another.

I didn't know where the swells were taking me. In fact, I suddenly realized I had only a vague notion of where I was. I hadn't been able to navigate since we had left the California coast. The only thing I knew for certain was that we had generally been heading west. I looked around and saw I was in a perfect circle, totally alone, and that the circle was moving with me as if it were a clear glass bowl. Every foot I moved, every yard I sailed, every mile that passed, the circle moved with me. This was my world. For the first time I didn't care where I was. I didn't even want to find land. I wanted to go on and on forever.

Of course, I knew that eventually I had to locate myself. After a while, I decided to see if I could take my first sun shot. I had my chronometer and my radio to tell me exactly what time it was. In another half hour, it would be noon. Because there was no Global Positioning System, or GPS, I took my sextant out of the box and began preparing for this most important event. As I looked through the eyepiece, I practiced bringing the sun down on the horizon, then checking to see the exact angle of the sun. When it was exact noon, I took my shot carefully and quickly. I wrote down the results and took out the book on navigation, got out all my charts and navigation tables, and went to work. It took me four hours to reduce my reading to latitude and longitude that first time.

I could hardly wait to look at the chart to see where I was. I was startled to find I was in the middle of the Nevada desert! It took me another two hours to come up with a more likely location. I found myself about eight hundred miles off the Mexican coast, way out of the shipping lanes. This didn't surprise me because we hadn't seen any other human activity or craft for the last seven or eight days. In fact, we didn't see a ship, a boat, a plane, or any other sign of human activity for another two weeks. During those two weeks, I could tell that each navigational check was finer and finer and, while I didn't know for sure, I felt I knew exactly where I was. That is a feeling I still have today.

The thought came to me again the next day. It was early in the morning. The sun was behind my back, the sky was a brilliant blue, and everything was ordered on the boat, with every rope coiled and the deck bristling clean. The deep green of the water hypnotized me as the gentle swells rolled under the boat. All of a sudden, a silver flash came screaming out of the deep green roller I was observing. At least ten large flying fish broke the surface and flew over the bow of the boat to disappear as quickly as they had come. The thought was as crystal as it was clear: "Those fish always know where they are, and so do I."

A week after the storm, we moved into balmy weather; it came down on us like an overcoat. Before the air was crisp, and all of a sudden we felt the warm, heavy air of the tropics. It was just phenomenal. We felt totally different. It was warm, and Gina was finally feeling better. We were sitting on the deck and letting the wind vane steering take over.

After we got into tropical waters, we had three days of squalls, which are mini-storms. I could look out on the horizon and see up to seven of them at a time. Sometimes we would manage to sail between them and sometimes we would hit them. Whenever we hit one, I had to reef the sails because the winds might be thirty to forty miles an hour. Because of this, I reefed the sails at night. A couple of nights later, I got up to check the wind vane. It was raining. I looked toward the horizon, and there was a moonbow, which I think I'd heard about in poetry but had never seen. A moonbow forms when it is rainy and cloudy with the moon right behind the squall. The incredible moonbow I saw that night was rich with mauve, purple, and pink. It was absolutely stunning. I just sat up there the whole watch to experience the event. With each passing day and night, my feeling of living in the moment became more meaningful.

As we entered tropical waters, we marveled at the incredible sea life. I felt at one with the sea. We were far from land, and there weren't any fishermen. The water was just boiling with fish. I took out a feather and a hook and about a hundred-pound test line and threw the line over. The mahi-mahi were simply fighting to see who got the hook. I pulled up a big thirty-pound mahi-mahi, which is pure white meat. Then I went through an exquisite hour of preparing the fish. I washed it very carefully, and every time I cut it with my knife, I would wipe the knife off so there'd be no fish oil on it whatsoever. I slowly filleted it to white chunks of meat. I went below and opened a fine bottle of wine. I was well stocked. Gina and I cooked and ate each piece individually as we drank a little wine. It was the best thing I have ever tasted. It was golden brown, totally moist, and totally fresh, an hour out of the water. I can still taste it today. In that setting, everything I did became incredibly beautiful. I realized that the meaning of our lives is in the details. The meaning doesn't have to do with trying to become someone, but in the present detail of the moment because there is no place else.

I was getting really good at using the sextant, and the lines started to get straight. One day we took a shot and put a dot on the map and thought we should be able to see land. I got out the binoculars and looked over the horizon. At first I couldn't see anything. I had never come across an ocean before, so of course I didn't know exactly what I was looking for. Finally, I saw what looked like a little circular cloud way off on the horizon. As we got closer, I saw a little dark space just above the water. Pretty soon I could tell it was an island. We came in at exactly the point on Maui that we were shooting for! We spent the next two months sailing around the Hawaiian Islands. As we explored the islands by boat, we saw them from a totally different vantage than the ordinary tourist. One time we were sailing on the lower islands. It was getting dark, and we pulled into a small cove. The cove was filled with boats, and I realized we were in the middle of a Japanese fishing fleet. The Japanese came over and brought beer and fruit; they wanted to hear all about our crossing the ocean. They were making a big deal about us crossing the ocean when they went out and risked their lives every day in their boats. It was quite an incredible and humbling experience to be with these fishermen.

At the end of the trip, we were in Kauai. My son Kyle was flying into Honolulu, so I flew over to meet him. During that flight, I had an interesting experience that taught me how much I had grown during the trip. For the past three months, I had been six feet above the water and had not gotten the perspective of the islands from above. It was a beautiful sunlit day, and I was totally fascinated as I looked out the window at all the harbors and places we had traveled by boat. I loved seeing the different colors of blue of the water and the greenery and beautiful density of the Hawaiian Islands.

As I looked out the window, I noticed a little disturbance in my ear. It was the voice of the woman sitting next to me, complaining about everything under the sun. Her complaints focused on picky little details about her kids, her car, and her husband. I was still looking out the window, but apparently she was talking to me. I finally turned to look at her, and I was amazed that this beautiful thirty-eight-year-old woman was complaining about all of this stuff.

I looked into her eyes and heard myself saying, "Let's play a game together and pretend that this plane has broken in half right in front of our seats. At this point, we have three choices: we can cling to our seats for the rest of our lives in stark terror, we can sit here and worry about all of the things we haven't done, or we can simply unbuckle our seatbelts, stand on the edge, jump off, and fly for the rest of our lives." My remark was greeted with dead silence, so I turned back around to resume looking out the window. I thoroughly enjoyed the rest of the flight.

Soon the plane landed, and as we were disembarking from the plane, the woman who'd been sitting next to me approached me, gave me a big hug, and thanked me profusely. My words had seeped in and changed her whole perspective on her life.

I could measure how much I'd grown and how different my perceptions were as I reflected on our exchange. My sailing adventure truly had shown me how to enjoy the adventure of life whatever the circumstances.

CHAPTER 25

Living in
Unearned Grace

In October 2002, I had a heart attack, which afforded me a rich opportunity to grow personally and to experience a great adventure. It was
an adventure I had never thought of taking, but it was really exciting. It
was like going to a foreign country, especially intensive care. In intensive
care, people speak in a different language and they eat horrible food. They
are like a colony of ants rushing about and doing their duty regardless of
how it affects you. It is a different and fascinating world. It is a totally different context. To give you the feel of the experience, I would like to share
some of the insights that came to me during my time in the hospital.

The Gift of Adversity

One of my favorite books is *Shogun* by James Clavell. This book tells
the story of an English captain and his crew who travel around the

Straits of Magellan in the Pacific and end up in Japan, where the only people besides the Japanese are the Portuguese and some Jesuit priests. The captain's ship wrecks, and he goes through a tremendous adventure. He does not know the language or the customs or when to bow. He does not even realize that a word of displeasure from him can cause a villager to lose his head. This world works on its own terms, but the captain is unfamiliar with it. This is how I felt in the hospital. As you know, I have crossed the ocean and I enjoy exploring. For me, the hospital was a strange new world to explore. And I encountered all kinds of personalities and all kinds of experiences in this new world.

While I was in the hospital, I had a strange dream that lasted approximately two weeks. The story of this dream was as real as me being here today. I would come out of the dream to eat and ask Lori if we had a life out in the world, and then I would go back into my dream. The adventure of the dream still amazes me. It was the most dramatic time in my life, but I didn't understand it for a long time. My life was on the line every minute for two weeks. It was a high adventure with many dangers and a significant enemy.

In the dream, I was on a huge peninsula in a different country. There was a metal gate that cut off the peninsula from the larger land mass. On the peninsula lived Indians who were treated as second-class citizens. My job was to figure out how to get them beyond the gate. They all wanted to get out and grow. The metal gate was heated and remained white-hot, preventing escape. The people would line up to impale and burn themselves on this gate in their attempts to break through and be free.

This is the price we all pay to be free. I am the Indian, and so are you. Part of us has to die to live. We have to give up our old selves, as well as our culture, history, and fears, to really break through and be free. In the dream, I was an outside observer trying to help, but as a little boy I was on the inside— I was a second-class citizen.

During the process of getting the Indians out the gate, I had to go through all kinds of intrigue. Every once in a while, I found myself in a situation where I had to lose my life. When that happened, I would just step out of my body and connect with a stream of white light that would come down. Then I would take a new lifeline. During my long dream, I experienced about thirty new lifelines. It was clear to me that these lifelines were always available to everyone. As I looked back on my life, I saw that every time I annihilated myself, in order to live again I would take a new lifeline. The way I see it now is that there is always a new lifeline for each of us if we are willing to walk away from the old one. A new lifeline is always there for us. It takes courage to go through our fears and to grab hold of new lifelines.

To really live in every aspect of our lives, we have to be willing to let go of our culture and our history. This doesn't mean we cannot learn from our history; it simply means that our history does not own us any longer.

As I look back, I realize that my life has been a series of annihilations. When my mother left me, it was an annihilation. When my brother and my father left me, these were annihilations. I had to be willing to leave the old before I could move on to the new. There is always a sacrifice in leaving the old. There are gains and losses, but everything is always perfect. None of the perils and drama that come into our lives really matter because we can always take a new lifeline whenever we want.

The Gift of Dropping Out of Life

Another meaningful experience I learned from my hospital stay was that I could easily drop out of life. This realization was a bit like dying and going to my own funeral. I dropped out of everything for five months, and for two of those months I saw practically no one. Life goes on as if you do not exist. I just unplugged and observed life for a few months. It was a little like my three-month journeys to remote places, only more so. It was fabulous, and I realized that any of us could do this anytime we wanted to. Life is a conveyor belt; we can either step on or off. It simply does not matter, and when we are ready to plug back in, we can. It is great to know we do not matter, that we can all take breaks in our lives at any time to regain our freedom. Truly, we can live our lives so that we feel the freedom of summer vacation every day.

After I got out of the hospital, I was in a wheelchair because my muscles had degenerated. Since they had cut my chest open, I wasn't supposed to lift anything over eight pounds. To amplify the adventure, I decided to recuperate and rehabilitate for a month at the Davenport Hotel in Spokane, Washington. This was a hundred-year-old elegant hotel that had just been remodeled. Being in a wheelchair in the hospital was different from being in a wheelchair at this fancy resort, because at the resort everyone seeing me thought that I was permanently disabled. So I had a whole new experience of being a disabled person in a wheelchair. Even though I was perfectly alert as Lori wheeled me around, nobody looked at me. At the restaurant, as I was sitting there in the wheelchair surveying the menu, the waiter would ask Lori what I wanted to eat. Even though I would say what I wanted, the waiter would still ask Lori, "Is that what he wants?" I found it great to be totally invisible in this way because I had no need to prove myself to be visible. When I first arrived at the hotel, I could barely walk eighty feet, but over the course of the month my body responded beautifully, and every day I grew stronger. When I started walking around the hotel, people started to talk to me.

When I got home, I stepped back into life again, but it was great to know that I could unplug and drop out at any time. One of the traps we fall into is thinking that we cannot get off the treadmill, when the truth is we can do it at any second. I am now physically healthier than I have been at any point in the past ten years, and I feel great. One of the things I appreciate most about life is that even when things have gotten completely crazy, I have always been able to take a new lifeline and create a new life.

Living in the Spiritual Realm

We always have a choice about whether to live our lives spiritually or materially. When the results are more important than how we go about getting them, we are living in the material realm. When the process is more important than the results, we are dwelling in the spiritual realm. The process *is* spirit. The first step to living in the spiritual realm is recognizing how material we are when we focus on pursuing end results. We claim our spirituality through intent, which is a feeling from the heart. Intent is not about discipline; it's about recognizing the inherent process that is most true for each of us, and allowing it to blossom.

The Concept of Self-Worth

Human civilization has taught us to live materially by emphasizing the concept of self-worth. We humans are part of the animal kingdom, but you never see other animals worrying about their self-worth! Self-worth is a human concept. Institutions such as governments and religions developed the idea of negative and positive self-worth to control the population and to get people to do what they want. Four centuries ago, the Native Americans had no concept of self-worth because they were just being themselves. They were strong individuals who took care of themselves and lived in process.

To be at peace with our daily lives requires changing our thinking and realizing that life is a process, not an end. As I've said before, if you don't enjoy the process, you're going to hate the end, which is death. Your children are also a process, not an end; if you don't enjoy the process, you're going to hate the end. Your business is a process, not an end; if you don't enjoy the process, you're going to hate the end. Your relationship is a process, not an end; if you don't enjoy the process, you're going to hate the end. So often we keep looking for the end result instead of enjoying the process. Because we never take time to live our lives deeply, they become shallow and hollow. Living in the process forces us to live in the moment. In reality, we have no choice but to live in the moment; the question is what we are doing with that moment. Many people spend their moments in worry or fear, which pulls of them out of the present.

Once I learned to accept the consequences of fear or worry, I opened to the possibilities of living freely and joyfully. It's okay to feel fear, and we gain our strength by facing the fear. Initially we have to face our fears heroically because we have not learned to accept all of the consequences. As we progress in the process, we find that the more we face our fears, the more this becomes like drinking a glass of water. It takes a great deal of practice, but eventually we do not even notice the fear. It begins to feel more like excitement rather than terror or paralysis. Horrid fear is a kind of resistance that entails a refusal to accept the unacceptable. When we focus on such fear, it limits us. In general, our world is a fairly safe place, and genuine fear is only necessary once or twice a year, if that. If we let go of all of our needless fears, we find we can live our lives in a very relaxed fashion and trust that we will be able to respond appropriately to any real peril.

The Gift of Gratitude

I have found that much of my happiness and joy comes from being aware and appreciative of everything that has come into my life. We Americans have been blessed with so many things that we take for granted, such as health, freedom, or just being born here. The odds of being born in the United States are millions to one. I call all of these great gifts unearned grace.

It is sad that so often we feel we have to earn our way each day to be worthy of these gifts. Let's accept the gifts that we have been given. It's rude even to consider repaying them because it is insulting to the giver to pay for a gift. Take time each day to be aware and appreciative of the gifts in your life. Being grateful for all the good and bad in our lives entails understanding that if it were not for the drama we've experienced, we would not be who we are today. This is the step before living in grace.

Although the right to the pursuit of happiness is in our U. S. Constitution, it is a total illusion. Happiness doesn't have anything to do with pursuing anything. We think if we get enough done or make enough money or if we have the right relationship, *then* we will be happy. This concept of happiness depends on an end result and is therefore part of the materialistic realm.

What we really want is to live well and to be fulfilled. The key to living in grace is being present in every moment, which is a spiritual concept connected to process, not result. Living in unearned grace comes from being totally grounded and owning and accepting who you are, knowing that you will take care of yourself and live in alignment with your self-interest. Each moment of the day becomes an adventure. Grace comes from the state of being in the moment. It reflects a steady groundedness in who you are and how you are going to respond. It entails a steady flow of engaging with life, beyond any confusion or dilemma. When you are grounded and perils arise, they become interesting. You don't get upset about them, but simply respond appropriately, without anger or fear. Life can seem boring without drama or perils. The turmoil in life gives you the opportunity to be creative and express yourself. Following this philosophy allows you to feel grounded, real, human, and solid. When people are not grounded, they see life happening to them instead of taking ownership and being totally responsible for themselves.

When I wake up in the morning, I start the day quietly and address the different events during my day through intent. As my day progresses, I watch my intent growing. I might feel good about the things I am doing or occasionally I might feel frustrated, but this doesn't take away from or add to my self-worth. The activity of the day is simply what I'm engaged in through my intent. I never let my activities be controlled by trying to prove my self-worth, which would only pull me out of the moment and away from appreciating the unearned grace that keeps my life abundant with great gifts.

Everyone is entitled to live a peaceful and joyous life without taking life seriously. We are only going to be on this planet a brief time, so why take anything too seriously? Right now we have everything we need in our lives to be happy and satisfied. The path to inner peace is learning to be in the moment and to accept what was, what is, and what might be.

Enjoy the process.

APPENDIX A

Exercises

Exercise 1 (Chapter 1):
Creating a Time and Money Journal

1. Please select a notebook or journal that appeals to you and label it "My Time and Money Journal." This journal will provide a place where you can jot down insights that occur to you as you read the book. Perhaps a story will remind you of choices you've made in your own life. You can note them here. Similarly, this is a good place to write about anything you decide you'd like to set in motion to put the principles into practice in your own life.

2. There are a number of exercises in this appendix, which I've referred to in the text at the appropriate places. Having your Time and Money Journal at hand will ensure that you derive the most benefit from doing them.

Exercise 2 (Chapter 4):
Writing Your Money Autobiography

1. Here's your chance to write your personal money autobiography. This autobiography will serve you best if it is a truthful account of significant life events relating to money. For example, your parents may have used money as a form of control, or they may have died and the money you live on came from their death. Look for your dominant money themes. Here are some examples of such themes:

You'll never have enough money.

Money is love.

You pretend money doesn't matter.

Making money is the driving force in your life.

Even though you may not have been aware of them before, these themes include the attitudes that affect your relationship with money. You'll be looking at every aspect of your relationship with money from childhood up until the present. The more you put into this exercise, the more you'll get out of it.

2. In your Time and Money Journal, briefly describe your mother's relationship with money, including her feelings. Now describe your father's relationship with money, including his feelings. Describe your mother's attitudes toward debt. Describe your father's attitudes toward debt.

3. Jot down some of the exact words your mother and father used with regard to money and debt. Be specific and complete, and include any concerns either of them expressed regarding what other people might think.

4. Describe any other people in your childhood who had an impact on your early imprinting around money or debt. What messages did you internalize from them?

5. Write a bit about how the messages you received in your childhood have affected your adult relationship with money.

6. Answer the following question: In what areas do you have integrity with money and in what areas are you out of integrity with money? An example of having integrity with money is that you have a game plan that is working so you are not anxious. The areas in your life where you are anxious about money point to the places where you are out of integrity with money. Explore the roots in your childhood.

7. Now, put the pieces together as a story. This is your money autobiography. Begin with your childhood, and you'll find that an organizational theme will emerge. Start with your very first experience with money. Then write about your particular money history, including any disasters, losses, good fortunes, or lucky wins that you have experienced.

Exercise 3 (Chapter 4):
Exploring Your Feelings about Money

1. Now that you've explored the basics of your money history, let's zoom in on the emotional component. List all of the negative and positive emotions you have concerning money and debt.

2. Describe the circumstances under which you experience each of the emotions you have just listed. Take the time to be thorough so you can understand these dynamics as deeply as possible.

3. Briefly describe how you would feel if you had unbelievable wealth and everyone knew it.

4. Discuss how you would feel if you lost all your money and were forced to go bankrupt and everyone knew it.

5. What are your ideas or plans with regard to money and debt? How do you feel about these plans? Make a chart in your Time and Money Journal and describe what actions you are currently taking—or comment on areas of inaction—with regard to each economic category listed here:

Real property

Liquid assets

Gambling fund

Earnings

Insurance

Savings

Debt

Consumption

Business plan

6. What positive or negative impact on your life would money have if you practiced complete integrity with every aspect of money? Write about your relationship with your family, your children, your business, and other significant areas as you answer this question. How does it feel to be aware of this?

Exercise 4 (Chapter 4): Transforming Your Relationship with Money

1. Now that you've explored some of your family imprints as well as your emotions around money, it's time for you to begin the process of taking back your power by transforming your relationship with money. You may wish to repeat the following exercise once you have read the entire book and have a deeper grasp of each of these areas.

2. Is it possible for you to experience abundance regardless of how much money you are making? If your answer is yes, write a paragraph that includes a description of how little money you could have and still feel abundant. If the answer is no, discuss your feelings and thoughts about this.

3. What are some of the feelings and attitudes you have about money and debt that you would like to modify? How motivated are you to change them?

4. In Exercise 3, you described the actions or areas of inaction with regard to a list of economic categories. Make another chart listing these categories in your Time and Money Journal, and on the new chart indicate your new game plan or intentions in each of the areas listed:

Real property

Liquid assets

Gambling fund

Earnings

Insurance

Savings

Debt

Consumption

Business plan

5. Write a bit about what it feels like to be coming into integrity with money.

Exercise 5 (Chapter 5):
Writing Your New Money Story

1. To write your new story, be sure to set aside a solid chunk of time in a quiet place. Ask yourself this question: "If I could have my life be any way I wanted it, how would I have it?" Close your eyes, and get a crystal-clear picture. See what your environment looks like, what your relationships look like, and what your home and office look like. Let yourself get a clear sense of the type of work you are doing, who you are doing it with, and what your income is.

2. Now take some time to write your story down in your Time and Money Journal. Write your story in the present tense, as if it is happening right now. Use affirmative language to write a detailed description that focuses on what you want, not on what you don't want. You may want to start by writing a list of all the elements that are meaningful in your life and why. Go deeply into the substance of your life. What do you want to do in your life before you die? This may include having love, abundance, good health, energy, peace, money, excitement, adventure, great sex, creativity, spontaneity, travel, freedom, independence, children you enjoy, contentment, time to enjoy yourself, surprise, growth, acceptance, unconditional love, laughter, learning, dance, reading, joy, safety, time just to be, altruistic service, and self-acceptance. If some of these ring true, be sure to incorporate them into your story.

3. Focus your story on the various areas of your life I've listed, but don't be limited to these. Look at your relationships, where you live, your work environment, your finances, and your physical and emotional health. Be sure to incorporate specific personal and financial visions into your story.

4. Once you have written your story to include these areas, test your story on a feeling level. Do you feel relaxed, happy, and maybe even excited as you read it? If you feel any lingering anxiety, explore the feeling; see if there's anything in your story that you want to modify so you'll feel in greater alignment with it.

Exercise 6 (Chapter 8):
Charting Your Assets and Debts and Mapping a Plan

1. Use a pencil to list of all of your personal and business debts on the Assets and Liabilities Chart in Appendix D. Include the name of the debt, the amount financed, the current balance due, your regular monthly payment, and the payoff date.

2. Use a pencil to list your income and expenses in the chart in Appendix C to help you develop ways of increasing your savings, freeing up money to pay off debts.

3. Now read the Summary of the Time and Money Game Plan in Appendix G, review the Time and Money Game Plan Diagram in Chapter 8, and go to the Time and Money Game Plan Worksheet in Appendix E, where you can map out your specific debt-reduction game plan.

4. Keep a copy of these charts in your Time and Money Journal and track your progress over time.

Exercise 7 (Chapter 11):
Rating Your Current Investments

1. In your Time and Money Journal, make a list of each one of your investments and major possessions, starting with those that rate a +10 on the investment scale and ending with those that rate a -10. Remember, high-quality, liquid assets that are safely invested in geometrically compounding tax-free or tax-deferred environments receive the highest scores.

2. Make note of the items that add meaning to your life but that may not meet the four basic criteria. Remember, it is fine to have these things and give them high ratings so long as they add meaning to your life, but make plans to convert them to safe liquid assets as soon as they lose meaning for you.

3. Except in cases where an investment brings significant meaning to your life, begin to identify ways to move an asset with lower ratings into cash and then reinvest it in one of your higher rated investments.

Exercise 8 (Chapter 15):
Preparing Your Document Locator and Final Wishes

1. Use the form in Appendix F to help you gather the information that will inform your loved ones where important papers are, what assets you have, and how they can contact your key advisors. You may wish to use your Time and Money Journal for your rough draft, then print clearly or type up the final version.

2. Make sure the members of your family have a copy of your completed list, and update it regularly. Conveying this information in a thorough form is one of the most loving and thoughtful gifts you can give your family; it will save them untold stress at a difficult time.

Exercise 9 (Chapter 20):
Clearing Out Physical Junk

1. In your Time and Money Journal, list all of your important possessions, large and small.

2. Now review your list. For each item, ask yourself, "Does this add meaning to my life?" If you find that some of the items on your list do not add meaning to your life, get rid of them. If you find that something is neutral, give it away. If you have something that you might use in the near future, then store it, but if you find you still haven't used it in six months, let it go.

3. You can first try to sell your junk, but if you can't sell it or don't enjoy the process of selling it, give it away. If you have something substantial that is hard to sell, you can always donate it to a charity and get a receipt so you can write it off on your income tax.

4. This is a good exercise to practice on a regular basis every six months. In this way, you'll keep your life free of physical clutter.

Exercise 10 (Chapter 20):
How You Spend Your Time

1. In your Time and Money Journal, list everything you spend your time on during the year. Include every single thing, from brushing your teeth and

going to the bathroom to sex, cleaning, grooming, eating, talking on the phone, cleaning house, shopping, and so on.

2. Number everything on the list beginning with what is most meaningful for you and ending with what is not meaningful at all. For each item on the list, ask yourself, "Does this add meaning to my life?"

3. Circle the items on your list that do not add meaning to your life.

4. Put a check mark next to anything on the list you would rather not be spending time on. Are there some items you could just stop doing? Are there others that someone else could do?

5. Begin the process of delegating the check-marked items to others. What would happen if you only spent time doing what you truly wanted to do?

Exercise 11 (Chapter 20):
Exploring Your Relationship with Yourself

1. The roles we play in life—whether as parent, child, teacher, lover, artist, activist, leader, or follower—can also fill our lives with time clutter. In this exercise, you'll get a chance to explore your relationship with yourself and the roles you play in life. In your Time and Money Journal, write your reflections on your relationship with yourself—body, mind, and spirit (essential aliveness).

2. List all of the roles you play in life, from the most meaningful to the least meaningful.

   a. Are there any roles you can eliminate? List them.

   b. Are there any roles you can make more meaningful? How?

3. List all of your hobbies, leisure activities, and interests, beginning with the most meaningful and ending with the least meaningful.

   a. Are there any you would like to eliminate?

   b. Are there any you could make more meaningful? How?

Exercise 12 (Chapter 20):
Exploring Your Relationships with Others

1. In your Time and Money Journal, list all the people you've spent time with during the past year. Begin your list with the people who have the most meaning in your life and end it with those who have little or no meaning.

2. Once your list is complete, draw a line through the list to break it into two groups. The people who add meaning to your life are above the line, and those who add little or no meaning are below the line.

3. For each person on your list, ask yourself the following questions and write the responses in your journal:

    a. "Why did I choose to spend time with this person?" Write one word that describes how you feel when you're around this person.

    b. "What would happen if I didn't spend time around this person?"

    c. If there are people who add little or no meaning to your life but with whom you have no choice but to spend time, ask yourself, "How could I change the context of this relationship so that it adds meaning to my life?"

4. Note in your journal any choices you've decided to make after doing this exercise.

Exercise 13 (Chapter 22): Simplifying Your Family's Life

1. In your Time and Money Journal, list all of the activities you do with your family, from the most meaningful to the least meaningful.

    a. Are there any you would like to eliminate?

    b. Are there any you could make more meaningful? How?

2. What aspects of your children's lives could be simplified? In other words, is it possible to eliminate activities, things, or relationships that don't add meaning to their lives or that interfere with your life?

3. How could you as a family find ways to spend more meaningful time together and eliminate aspects that aren't so meaningful? How could you and your partner create more meaningful time together? Begin today to make the changes that simplify your family's life and make your time together more meaningful.

APPENDIX B

Saving Charts Showing Geometric Progression

$30,000 Income	Tax-Deferred Savings			Year	Tax-Deferred Savings		
Year	Annual savings	Beginning balance	Interest 6.00%	Ending Balance		Beginning balance	Interest 8.00%	Ending balance
1	$12,000	$12,000	$720	$12,720	1	$12,000	$960	$12,960
2	12,000	24,720	1,483	26,203	2	24,960	1,997	26,957
3	12,000	38,203	2,292	40,495	3	38,957	3,117	42,073
4	12,000	52,495	3,150	55,645	4	54,073	4,326	58,399
5	12,000	67,645	4,059	71,704	5	70,399	5,632	76,031
6	12,000	83,704	5,022	88,726	6	88,031	7,042	95,074
7	12,000	100,726	6,044	106,770	7	107,074	8,566	115,640
8	12,000	118,770	7,126	125,896	8	127,640	10,211	137,851
9	12,000	137,896	8,274	146,170	9	149,851	11,988	161,839
10	12,000	158,170	9,490	167,660	10	173,839	13,907	187,746
11	12,000	179,660	10,780	190,439	11	199,746	15,980	215,726
12	12,000	202,439	12,146	214,586	12	227,726	18,218	245,944
13	12,000	226,586	13,595	240,181	13	257,944	20,635	278,579
14	12,000	252,181	15,131	267,312	14	290,579	23,246	313,825
15	12,000	279,312	16,759	296,070	15	325,825	26,066	351,891
16	12,000	308,070	18,484	326,555	16	363,891	29,111	393,003
17	12,000	338,555	20,313	358,868	17	405,003	32,400	437,403
18	12,000	370,868	22,252	393,120	18	449,403	35,952	485,355
19	12,000	405,120	24,307	429,427	19	497,355	39,788	537,144
20	12,000	441,427	26,486	467,913	20	549,144	43,931	593,075
21	12,000	479,913	28,795	508,707	21	605,075	48,406	653,481
22	12,000	520,707	31,242	551,950	22	665,481	53,238	718,720
23	12,000	563,950	33,837	597,787	23	730,720	58,458	789,177
24	12,000	609,787	36,587	646,374	24	801,177	64,094	865,271
25	12,000	658,374	39,502	697,877	25	877,271	70,182	947,453
26	12,000	709,877	42,593	752,469	26	959,453	76,756	1,036,209
27	12,000	764,469	45,868	810,337	27	1,048,209	83,857	1,132,066
28	12,000	822,337	49,340	871,678	28	1,144,066	91,525	1,235,591
29	12,000	883,678	53,021	936,698	29	1,247,591	99,807	1,347,399
30	12,000	948,698	56,922	1,005,620	30	1,359,399	108,752	1,468,150
31	12,000	1,017,620	61,057	1,078,677	31	1,480,150	118,412	1,598,562
32	12,000	1,090,677	65,441	1,156,118	32	1,610,562	128,845	1,739,407
33	12,000	1,168,118	70,087	1,238,205	33	1,751,407	140,113	1,891,520
34	12,000	1,250,205	75,012	1,325,217	34	1,903,520	152,282	2,055,802
35	12,000	1,337,217	80,233	1,417,450	35	2,067,802	165,424	2,233,226

$100,000 Income		Tax-Deferred Savings		°	°	Tax-Deferred Savings		
Year	Annual savings	Beginning balance	Interest 6.00%	Ending Balance	Year	Beginning balance	Interest 8.00%	Ending balance
1	$40,000	$40,000	$2,400	$42,400	1	$40,000	$3,200	$43,200
2	40,000	82,400	4,944	87,344	2	83,200	6,656	89,856
3	40,000	127,344	7,641	134,985	3	129,856	10,388	140,244
4	40,000	174,985	10,499	185,484	4	180,244	14,420	194,664
5	40,000	225,484	13,529	239,013	5	234,664	18,773	253,437
6	40,000	279,013	16,741	295,754	6	293,437	23,475	316,912
7	40,000	335,754	20,145	355,899	7	356,912	28,553	385,465
8	40,000	395,899	23,754	419,653	8	425,465	34,037	459,502
9	40,000	459,653	27,579	487,232	9	499,502	39,960	539,462
10	40,000	527,232	31,634	558,866	10	579,462	46,357	625,819
11	40,000	598,866	35,932	634,798	11	665,819	53,266	719,085
12	40,000	674,798	40,488	715,286	12	759,085	60,727	819,812
13	40,000	755,286	45,317	800,603	13	859,812	68,785	928,597
14	40,000	840,603	50,436	891,039	14	968,597	77,488	1,046,085
15	40,000	931,039	55,862	986,901	15	1,086,085	86,887	1,172,971
16	40,000	1,026,901	61,614	1,088,515	16	1,212,971	97,038	1,310,009
17	40,000	1,128,515	67,711	1,196,226	17	1,350,009	108,001	1,458,010
18	40,000	1,236,226	74,174	1,310,400	18	1,498,010	119,841	1,617,851
19	40,000	1,350,400	81,024	1,431,424	19	1,657,851	132,628	1,790,479
20	40,000	1,471,424	88,285	1,559,709	20	1,830,479	146,438	1,976,917
21	40,000	1,599,709	95,983	1,695,692	21	2,016,917	161,353	2,178,270
22	40,000	1,735,692	104,141	1,839,833	22	2,218,270	177,462	2,395,732
23	40,000	1,879,833	112,790	1,992,623	23	2,435,732	194,859	2,630,590
24	40,000	2,032,623	121,957	2,154,580	24	2,670,590	213,647	2,884,238
25	40,000	2,194,580	131,675	2,326,255	25	2,924,238	233,939	3,158,177
26	40,000	2,366,255	141,975	2,508,231	26	3,198,177	255,854	3,454,031
27	40,000	2,548,231	152,894	2,701,124	27	3,494,031	279,522	3,773,553
28	40,000	2,741,124	164,467	2,905,592	28	3,813,553	305,084	4,118,637
29	40,000	2,945,592	176,736	3,122,327	29	4,158,637	332,691	4,491,328
30	40,000	3,162,327	189,740	3,352,067	30	4,531,328	362,506	4,893,835
31	40,000	3,392,067	203,524	3,595,591	31	4,933,835	394,707	5,328,541
32	40,000	3,635,591	218,135	3,853,727	32	5,368,541	429,483	5,798,025
33	40,000	3,893,727	233,624	4,127,350	33	5,838,025	467,042	6,305,067
34	40,000	4,167,350	250,041	4,417,391	34	6,345,067	507,605	6,852,672
35	40,000	4,457,391	267,443	4,724,835	35	6,892,672	551,414	7,444,086

Time and Money: Your Guide to Economic Freedom

$250,000 Income	Tax-Deferred Savings		°	°	Tax-Deferred Savings		
Year	Annual savings	Beginning balance	Interest 6.00%	Ending Balance	Year	Beginning balance	Interest 8.00%	Ending balance
1	$100,000	$100,000	$6,000	$106,000	1	$100,000	$8,000	$108,000
2	100,000	206,000	12,360	218,360	2	208,000	16,640	224,640
3	100,000	318,360	19,102	337,462	3	324,640	25,971	350,611
4	100,000	437,462	26,248	463,709	4	450,611	36,049	486,660
5	100,000	563,709	33,823	597,532	5	586,660	46,933	633,593
6	100,000	697,532	41,852	739,384	6	733,593	58,687	792,280
7	100,000	839,384	50,363	889,747	7	892,280	71,382	963,663
8	100,000	989,747	59,385	1,049,132	8	1,063,663	85,093	1,148,756
9	100,000	1,149,132	68,948	1,218,079	9	1,248,756	99,900	1,348,656
10	100,000	1,318,079	79,085	1,397,164	10	1,448,656	115,892	1,564,549
11	100,000	1,497,164	89,830	1,586,994	11	1,664,549	133,164	1,797,713
12	100,000	1,686,994	101,220	1,788,214	12	1,897,713	151,817	2,049,530
13	100,000	1,888,214	113,293	2,001,507	13	2,149,530	171,962	2,321,492
14	100,000	2,101,507	126,090	2,227,597	14	2,421,492	193,719	2,615,211
15	100,000	2,327,597	139,656	2,467,253	15	2,715,211	217,217	2,932,428
16	100,000	2,567,253	154,035	2,721,288	16	3,032,428	242,594	3,275,023
17	100,000	2,821,288	169,277	2,990,565	17	3,375,023	270,002	3,645,024
18	100,000	3,090,565	185,434	3,275,999	18	3,745,024	299,602	4,044,626
19	100,000	3,375,999	202,560	3,578,559	19	4,144,626	331,570	4,476,196
20	100,000	3,678,559	220,714	3,899,273	20	4,576,196	366,096	4,942,292
21	100,000	3,999,273	239,956	4,239,229	21	5,042,292	403,383	5,445,676
22	100,000	4,339,229	260,354	4,599,583	22	5,545,676	443,654	5,989,330
23	100,000	4,699,583	281,975	4,981,558	23	6,089,330	487,146	6,576,476
24	100,000	5,081,558	304,893	5,386,451	24	6,676,476	534,118	7,210,594
25	100,000	5,486,451	329,187	5,815,638	25	7,310,594	584,848	7,895,442
26	100,000	5,915,638	354,938	6,270,577	26	7,995,442	639,635	8,635,077
27	100,000	6,370,577	382,235	6,752,811	27	8,735,077	698,806	9,433,883
28	100,000	6,852,811	411,169	7,263,980	28	9,533,883	762,711	10,296,594
29	100,000	7,363,980	441,839	7,805,819	29	10,396,594	831,727	11,228,321
30	100,000	7,905,819	474,349	8,380,168	30	11,328,321	906,266	12,234,587
31	100,000	8,480,168	508,810	8,988,978	31	12,334,587	986,767	13,321,354
32	100,000	9,088,978	545,339	9,634,316	32	13,421,354	1,073,708	14,495,062
33	100,000	9,734,316	584,059	10,318,375	33	14,595,062	1,167,605	15,762,667
34	100,000	10,418,375	625,103	11,043,478	34	15,862,667	1,269,013	17,131,680
35	100,000	11,143,478	668,609	11,812,087	35	17,231,680	1,378,534	18,610,215

APPENDIX C

Income and Expense Categories Chart

CATEGORIES	CURRENT	INCREASE	FOUND MONEY
Income			
Bonus			
Income tax return			
Salary			
Spouse salary			
Retirement income			
Stock dividends			
Tax-free interest			
Other			
		Total	$

EXPENSES	CURRENT	DECREASE	FOUND MONEY
Automobile			
Fuel			
License, tax			
Service			

EXPENSES	CURRENT	DECREASE	FOUND MONEY
Bank charges			
Business expenses			
Cable TV			
Cash			
Charity			
Cash contributions			
Noncash			
Child care			
Cleaners			
Clothing			
Country club			
Dining out			
Education			
Entertainment			
Gifts			
Groceries			
Haircuts			
Health care			
Health club			
Home repair			
Housing			
Mortgage/rent			
House cleaning			
Security			
Taxes			
Yard work			
Insurance			
Auto			
Home			
Life			
Medical			
Investments			
IRA contributions			
Self			
Spouse			
Medical/dental			

EXPENSES	CURRENT	DECREASE	FOUND MONEY
Medical			
Dental			
Chiropractic			
Medicine			
Miscellaneous			
Movie rentals			
Online services			
Parking, tolls			
Pet food & care			
Postage			
Recreation			
Retail Stores			
Retirement contrib.			
Savings			
Sports (golf, tennis, etc.)			
Subscriptions			
Supplies			
Taxes			
IRS			
Property			
State			
Telephone			
Home			
Cellular			
Travel			
TV & cable			
Utilities			
Gas & electric			
Water/sewer			
		Total	$
Total Found Money			$

APPENDIX D

Assets and Liabilities Chart

Assets	Amount	Liabilities (debts)	Amount
Cash		**Past-due obligations** (back taxes)	
Stocks and bonds		**Small debt** (under $10,000)	
Treasuries		Credit card	
Tax-free municipals			
Mutual funds			
Stocks			
Cash-value insurance			
		Other consumer debt	
Notes receivable		Auto loan balance	
Real estate		Small student loans	
Main home			
Vacation home		**Large debt (over $10,000)**	
		Auto loan balance	
Retirement plans		Home mortgage	
Defined benefit plan		Second mortgage	
401(k)		Lines of credit	
Roth IRAs			
Traditional IRAs			
SEP-IRAs			
Value of your work retirement		**Long-term debt**	
		Business loans	
Other assets & property		Student loans (over $10,000)	
Automobiles/boat			
Personal property			
Business			
Business value			
Business real estate		**Total liabilities $**	
Total assets $		**Net worth $**	

Time and Money Game Plan Worksheet

Payoff order	Liabilities/debt (phase)	Amount	Monthly payment	Added payment	Payoff Date
A	**Past-due obligations**				
	Back taxes				
B	**Small debt (under $10,000)**				
	Credit card				
	Other consumer debt				
	Auto loan balance				
	Small student loans				
C	**Roth IRA/pension** (*matching funds only*)			N/A	N/A
D	**Large debt (over $10,000)**				
	Auto loan balance				
	Home mortgage				
	Second mortgage				
	Lines of credit				
E-50%	**Savings**			N/A	N/A
	Tax-free municipal bonds			N/A	N/A
	Money market account			N/A	N/A
	Planned consumption			N/A	N/A
E-50%	**Long-term debt**				
	Business loans				
	Student loans (over $10,000)				

APPENDIX F

Document Locator and Final Wishes Chart

Insurance documents: _____

Birth certificates: _____

Deeds and proof of ownership: _____

Marriage license or certificate: _____

Social Security card(s): _____

Military records: _____

Divorce decree: _____

Mortgage documents: _____

Bank passbooks: _____

Passports: _____

Tax returns: _____

Wills and trusts: _____

Prenuptial agreement: _____

Business papers: _____

Death certificate of deceased spouse: _____

Warranties: _____

Stock certificates: _____

Other investment certificates: _____

Letters of final wishes: _____

Citizenship papers: _____

Safe-deposit keys: _____

Financial records: _____

Notification List

Accountant: _____

Attorney: _____

Banker: _____

Clergy: _____

Executor: _____

Contingent executor: _____

Funeral director: _____

Guardian: _____

Contingent guardian: _____

Insurance agent: _____

Insurance underwriter: _____

Life Insurance/Pension Data

Life insurance policies

Company: _____

Agent: _____ Telephone number: _____

Amount: _____ Date: _____

Location of policy: _____

Beneficiaries: _____

Company: _____

Agent: _____ Telephone number: _____

Amount: _____ Date: _____

Location of policy: _____

Beneficiaries: _____

Company: _____

Agent: _____ Telephone number: _____

Amount: _____ Date: _____

Location of policy: _____

Beneficiaries: _____

Accidental death benefits (for example, from purchasing an airline ticket with a credit card):

Carrier:

Terms of benefits:

Beneficiaries:

Pensions/Annuities

Company:

Contact: Telephone:

Company:

Contact: Telephone:

Personal Information

Full legal name:

Address:

Social Security number:

Spouse's Social Security number:

Medicare number:

Armed forces service number:

Date and location of discharge:

Birth date: Marriage date:

Father's full name:

Mother's full maiden name:

Widowed: Separated: Divorced: Date:

Location of separation agreement/divorce decree:

Remarried?   Yes   No   Date:

Children:

Name	Address	Birth date

Close friends

Name	Address	Phone

Wills

Location of original last will:

Date of will:

Location of any documents mentioned in will:

Funeral/Memorial Requests

Funeral home:

Director: Telephone:

Address:

Type of service: Religious: Military: Fraternal: Other:

Person officiating: Telephone:

Music selection:

Reading selection:

Flowers:

Memorials:

Pallbearers:

Burial or cremation:

If burial:

Cemetery:

Location:

Section: Plot number: Block:

Location of deed:

Special instructions:

If cremation:

Location to inter ashes:

Place to scatter ashes:

Other instructions:

Coverage of funeral expenses

Life insurance:

Social Security: Veteran's Administration:

Union benefits: Fraternal organizations:

Pension benefit:

Burial insurance:

APPENDIX G

Summary of the Time and Money Game Plan

1. First, evaluate where you stand financially. Fill out a financial report to determine your assets, liabilities, and net worth (see Appendix D). If you do not know where you're starting from, it's hard to determine what you need to do to get to the goal line of economic freedom.

2. Look at your entire investment portfolio and identify the stocks and mutual funds that you do not want to hold on to (see Exercise 7 in Appendix A). I recommend that you sell all stocks and place the money in safe, liquid assets where you never lose your principal and always have a specific rate of return.

3. Write down all of your monthly expenses (see Appendix C) to help you identify the "found money" that you can use to increase your savings and pay off debt.

4. Set up an automatic payroll deduction to go directly into your debt reduction savings account.

5. Clarify your new context and write a new personal money story for your life (see Exercise 5 in Appendix A). Write down your goals for increasing income, reducing debt, and increasing savings (see Chapter 5).

6. Reduce your spending, and increase your income and savings.

7. Set a specific dollar goal for paying off debt each month. As you pay off debt, your goal can increase as you use the "found money" that was going to monthly payments on debts that you have now paid off. Pay off all back taxes, credit cards, and consumer debt by following the Time and Money Game Plan Diagram in Chapter 8. Organize all of your debt into payoff phases using the worksheet in Appendix E.

8. Do the numbers. Write out all your debt along with your plan for paying off that debt. To see that it is really possible, note the exact date when you will be debt free. Update these numbers monthly.

9. Pay off all debt of $10,000 or less, starting with the smallest one first, while continuing to pay the minimum amount on all other debt. Once you see that you can pay off one debt, it will strengthen your resolve to continue. Once you have paid off that debt, go to the next smallest debt, adding on the additional money you freed up by paying off the first debt.

10. After you have paid off all of your small debt, take the additional money from the normal monthly payments that used to go to the small debt and maximize contributions to any matched pension plan fund at work along with your personal Roth IRA.

11. If you are a business owner and your pension plan is costing you more than 10 to 12 percent in administration fees and employee contributions, consider discontinuing the plan and investing that money in tax-free municipal bonds (see Chapter 11 and Chapter 12).

12. Now pay off your large debt (greater than $10,000). Once you have paid off your home and other large debt, divide your money between paying off long-term debt (such as business loans and large student

loans) and savings, which you'll be investing in tax-free municipal bonds. The average rate of return on tax-free municipal bonds has been around 6 percent. If bond interest rates are low (below 5.5 percent), put your money toward debt reduction. If interest rates are between 5.5 percent and 7 percent, divide your money equally between investing in bonds and paying off long-term debt. If interest rates are high (above 7 percent), invest two-thirds in tax-free municipal bonds and use the remaining one-third toward debt reduction. You will be surprised at how much excess money is available once you have a solid story of economic abundance.

13. If you have an emergency where you need to pay for a car repair or unexpected medical bills, or if you just feel you need a vacation, you can skip a month or two of debt reduction and use the freed-up cash to cover it. Then get back on track right away.

14. Once you have paid off all of your debt, celebrate. Know that you own your own home. You have funded your retirement plan, and have at least 40 to 50 percent of your income that you can put into tax-free municipal bonds. You are safely on your way to economic freedom.

15. Find a good accountant and broker who will listen to your desires and support and follow your game plan (see Chapter 12 for broker selection criteria and Appendix H for bond criteria).

16. Educate yourself in basic investing. Review this book, and use other reliable sources, such as the Recommended Resources listed in Appendix I.

17. Make your final wishes known by completing the form in Appendix F. Make sure you have a will, a revocable living trust, and durable power of attorney for financial and health-care matters.

18. Annually review your assets, write out the numbers, and update your game plan for financial abundance.

19. Use Part Two of this book as your inspiration and simplify your life. Decide to do only what you truly want to do, and let go of the rest.

20. Enjoy the day-to-day process of your life, knowing that you are safely on the road to economic freedom.

APPENDIX H

Criteria for Investing in Tax-Free Municipal Bonds

BOND CRITERIA	EXPLANATIONS
Bond safety	Buy tax-free municipal bonds that have an underlying quality credit rating of AA or better before insurance.
State of origin	First consider buying municipal bonds issued by municipalities within the state where you reside. If you do not have state income tax, you can buy from any state.
Type of bonds	Buy only general obligation or essential purpose revenue bonds.

BOND CRITERIA	EXPLANATIONS
Bonds to avoid	Stay away from housing bonds, hospital bonds, and any bonds associated with troubled industries, such as nuclear power or any controversial project. Avoid deeply discounted municipal bonds because of the income tax implications, where you could pay an escalated income tax rate on a capital gain portion of these bonds. Avoid any heavily premium bonds with short call features if it affects the yield to call. Do not buy bond funds or bond trusts.
Bond maturity	Buy bonds where the yield rate starts to flatten, usually around ten to twenty years. If the rate is lower than 5.5 percent, stay at around five to eight years. If rates are greater than 7 percent, go closer to twenty years.
Bond price	Bonds can be bought at face value (par), at a premium (above face value), or at discount (below face value). Premium bonds have an above-market yield (coupon), so you pay more than face value to get them. Always ask about the yield to worse call and compare this to other par bonds in the market.
Call feature	The call feature allows the issuer to buy the bonds back before the maturity date if interest rates drop; this protects the issuer.
Where to buy	Buy municipal bonds from long-established, large brokerage firms, such as A. G. Edwards and Sons, Smith Barney, Merrill Lynch, Charles Schwab, Paine Webber, Morgan Stanley, and Edward Jones, or a bond specialty firm, such as Griffin, Kubik, Stephens & Thompson out of Chicago, which only sells tax-free municipal bonds. These large firms will usually have the largest inventory, the highest expertise, and the greatest level of safety. Only work with firms that are registered with the National Association of Security Dealers (NASD) and that are insured by Security Investor Protection Corporation, which gives you at least $500,000 or more of protection.

APPENDIX I

Recommended Resources

Alexander, Michael A. *Stock Cycles* (iUniverse, 2000).

Clason, George S. *The Richest Man in Babylon* (Signet, 2002).

Cummuta, John M. *Are You Being Seduced into Debt?* (Nelson Books, 2004).

———. *Turn Your Debt into Wealth: A Proven System for Real Financial Freedom* (Simon & Schuster Audio, 2001).

Orman, Suze. *The Nine Steps to Financial Freedom* (Crown, 1997).

———. *The Courage to Be Rich* (video, 1998).

———. *The Road to Wealth* (Riverhead, 2001).

———. *Suze Orman's Financial Guidebook* (Three Rivers Press, 2002).

Stanley, Greg. *The Whitehall Financial Freedom Tapes* (Whitehall Management, 2001; phone: 623 934-2108; www.whitehallmgt.com/).

———. *Municipal Bonds: How and Why to Buy Them* (Whitehall Management, 2003).

———. *Stocks: Buy, Sell, or Hold?* (Whitehall Management, 2002).

———. *Stocks: Stay In or Get Out* (Whitehall Management, 2003).

———. *The Twenty-Five Real Reasons Why You Don't Save Money* (Whitehall Management, 2003).

Vick, Timothy P. *How to Pick Stocks Like Warren Buffet* (McGraw-Hill, 2000).

To order individual or bulk copies of this book at a discount or to see other books by ACG Press, go online at www.ACGPress.com

For information about Kendrick Mercer and the Garden Company's programs, books, and tapes, we invite you to visit the Garden Company website at http://www.gardenco.com

Garden Company
525 Pine Street
Sandpoint, ID 83864
Phone: 208-263-4586
Fax: 208-263-4630

Index

References to charts, tables, and exercises are in **bold type**.

Index

Index

Index